Research On
Open Innovation

**A collection of papers on Open Innovation
from leading researchers in the field**

An Openforum Academy Publication

Research On Open Innovation

Table of Contents

An Introduction to
'Research On Open Innovation'

By Andrew Updegrove

Once upon a time, the learned of the world willingly shared Great Ideas and discoveries among themselves, both nationally in scientific societies, and internationally through letters, often composed in Latin, the *lingua franca* of the recently enlightened Europe of that time. The resulting advancement in a broad range of scientific disciplines was prodigious, reaping enormous benefits we still enjoy today.

Or, at least, that's how the idealised version goes, and in fact much invaluable information was shared one-on-one among the great theoreticians and investigators of the time. But this was also the age of the Guilds, which jealously guided their knowledge, and later on of the era in which Darwin sat on his revolutionary theories for decades. He was only   startled into expedited disclosure when he received a letter from a young species collector named Alfred Russel Wallace, who was seeking the great man's opinion of Wallace's more high level, but otherwise consistent theory of evolution.

In truth, there has always been a tension between the making of a discovery and the where, when and how of its sharing. Sometimes brilliant innovations are kept secret, and used for the sole commercial benefit of their discoverers. Other times their description in a respected, peer-reviewed publication is the ultimate goal. And in many cases the sharing of the discovery is only allowed to occur after it has been protected as completely as possible under patent law – a slow and time-consuming process. The result in each case is that the advance of knowledge and the benefits for society that can follow materialise in a jerky, delayed fashion.

And yet in virtually every case discoveries are based upon the prior revelations of others – as Newton graciously phrased it, discerned only because the discoverer stood on the shoulders of the giants that came before. But what if all research, all experimental results, and all theories, were exposed to the world immediately?

The enormous benefits that such a practice could provide are almost beyond estimation. Not only might new cures for diseases be discovered and deployed more rapidly, but fewer billions of research dollars and countless hours of research time might be wasted if failed tests, as well as successful ones, were reliably and promptly reported, rather than never disclosed at all. Not only could science advance more quickly, but the return on foundation and tax dollars could be immeasurably greater as the same funds were redeployed to more productive use.

With the advent of the Internet as well as almost infinite, cheap computing power, the ability to capitalise on all forms of "openness" – in data sets, in research results, in source code, and more – and to benefit from the results has become too large to ignore. The degree to which innovation could broaden and accelerate in such an environment is almost limitless. Equally powerfully, the degree to which data and discoveries can be turned into products and services would provide an economic acceleration that governments, particularly in Europe, are beginning to realise and embrace.

Proponents of proprietary information, systems and code might scoff that such a vision is simply another idealised conception of scientific reality. But they would be wrong, and that is what this book, the third in OpenForum Europe's continuing series of books on all things open, is all about.

Unlike the prior anthologies in this series, which primarily included essays, 'Research On Open Innovation' compiles full length research papers by respected experts in their fields. In each case, the authors take a detailed, thoroughly referenced look into an area of scientific, commercial, legal or policy importance. In some cases, the authors investigate a single scientific discipline or industry sector, such as chemistry or communications. In others, they explore a foundational element, like intellectual property licensing, or practice, such as government procurement. Taken together, the findings presented in these papers begin to fill in the details of what a true open innovation-based ecosystem should look like, and how it would operate.

In reading the work of these authors, it is to be hoped that you will begin to think of ways that open access could accelerate your own work, whatever it may be. And also about how much more that work could be leveraged by others, if you were to embrace the same commitment to openness.

Not surprisingly, this book has been made available as a free download. We encourage you to visit the OpenForum Europe Web site, http://www.openforumeurope.org/ to learn more about what the Forum seeks to achieve in Europe, and about how you can help advance the goal of openness wherever in the world you may live.

Andrew Updegrove is a co-founder and partner of the Boston law firm of Gesmer Updegrove LLP. Since 1988 he has served as legal counsel to over 135 standards development organisations and open source foundations, most of which he has helped structure and launch. He has been retained by many of the largest technology companies in the world to assist them in forming such organisations.

He has also written and spoken extensively on the topics of consortia, standard setting and open source software, has given testimony to the United States Department of Justice, Federal Trade Commission, and Congressional and State legislative committees on the same topics, and has filed "friend of the court" briefs on a pro bono basis with the Federal Circuit Court, Supreme Court, and Federal Trade Commission in support of standards development in leading standards-related litigation. In 2002, he launched ConsortiumInfo.org, a website intended to be the most detailed and comprehensive resource on the Internet on the topics of consortia and standard setting, as well as Standards Today, a bi-monthly eJournal of news, ideas and analysis in the standard setting and open source areas with over 7,000 subscribers around the world. In 2005, he launched the Standards Blog. ConsortiumInfo.org serves over 10 million page views annually.

He has been a member of the United States Standards Strategy revision committee, and received the President's Award for Journalism from American National Standards Institute (ANSI) in 2005. His current and past Board service includes the Boards of Directors of ANSI, the Linux Foundation and the Free Standards Group, and the Boards of Advisors of HL7 and Open Source for America. He is a graduate of Yale University and the Cornell University Law School.

Architecting The Future Of Research Communication: Building The Models And Analytics For An Open Access Future

By Cameron Neylon[1]

We live in an exciting time. There are huge opportunities starting to open up for more effective research communication. The massive progress towards Open Access [1] is a core part of this. At the same time, the tools we have to display, manipulate, and interact with this content have become not just incredibly powerful, but easier to use. And as the web in general provides new kinds of services, new ways of communicating, telling stories, and manipulating data there is a profound cultural shift occurring as our expectations of what should be possible, indeed what should be easy, grow.

But as this vista opens up, we also have to make choices. The possibilities are multiplying but where should we focus our attention? More particularly, in a world of limited research resources where are the most important opportunities for greater efficiency? The Open Access movement has changed from a small community advocating for change, with successes in specific disciplines, to the centre of research policy making. But

---

[1] Reprinted from Neylon, C. (2013) PLOS Biology 11(10): e1001691. The text is subject to a Creative Commons Attribution 2.0 licence. The original text can be found at http://dx.doi.org/10.1371/journal.pbio.1001691 and the full licence can be consulted at http://creativecommons.org/licenses/by/2.0/

as we move into implementation, disagreements on details and priorities come to the surface.

These choices and the attendant disagreements are important and will occupy our attention for the next few years. But we also need to look beyond them. We need to ask ourselves what our overall priorities are for research and research communication. And we need a framework that we can use to critique the opportunities and costs that will arise as we look to extend the principles of Open Access from articles to books, grey literature, data, and materials, indeed to all the outputs of research. Increasingly researchers, institutions, and funders will be asking the question: with these resources for communication, how do I maximise the value of this research? Understanding how to answer these questions is possibly the core challenge for the next decade of scholarly communications. To meet this challenge we will need better frameworks to understand how scholarly communication works in a networked environment.

Open Content And Open Resources

As the process of implementing Open Access accelerates, it is worth reflecting on the varied underlying arguments for it. To maximise the benefits of Open Access we must first articulate what those benefits are, which ones we are prioritising, which are complementary, and which may pull against each other.

The Wider Access Argument

The first and simplest argument for widening access is that the taxpaying public deserves access to the outputs of the research they fund. This is a powerful argument; one that is easy to express and one that policy makers and politicians find compelling. The argument comes in broadly three variants (See Box 1): reducing the inefficiencies and redundancies that arise when researchers themselves can't access the literature; access for the general public and taxpayer; and access for translators and public engagement specialists who help to communicate research to the wider community.

Box 1. The Three Variants of the Access Argument

The first and simplest argument for widening access is that the taxpaying public deserves access to the outputs of the research they fund. This argument is most effective when it concerns areas of research that are of obvious public interest: for example, medical science, environmental science, economics, as well as history, literature, and languages. This argument focuses on people, and on reading, and it places the onus of developing an understanding of the research on the user.

A variant of this line of reasoning focuses on researchers themselves, who often have limited access to research literature. Funders, institutions, and researchers see the costs in time wasted looking for information and unknowingly repeating research. Outside the academic world, governments are increasingly concerned about how the lack of access affects small and medium enterprises (SMEs), with studies suggesting that the cost in lost time and sales to SMEs is substantial [10].

A development of this argument focuses on enabling greater comprehension, either of specific issues or of science itself, and on ensuring that those who can translate, interpret, and re-use research outputs have access to them. With improved access and ability to incorporate parts of research papers in their writing, bloggers, journalists, and public information providers are better

---

equipped to provide the layer of interpretation and synthesis that informs the wider public.

Each of these arguments tends to focuses only on access for reading. It is only when we consider the needs to interpreters and synthesisers that we see a need to enable the re-use of articles. Some argue that it is only the transmission of ideas that matter and that re-use rights are not important. I disagree with this viewpoint profoundly. The ideas may be enough for skilled interpreters in specific contexts, but permitting re-use enables a much larger group of people, and a much larger range of spaces, to aid in this synthesis. The biggest single opportunity for engaging the public with research is Wikipedia, the top hit for virtually any factual web search, and containing a set of sites that have more visitors in a day than most scholarly publishers receive in a year. Expending effort on local engagement efforts while failing to make research available and incorporated in Wikipedia will frequently be the wrong use of resources.

But all of these arguments focus on an individual user and thus they have a weakness. They don't truly recognise the benefits that arise collectively from the development of the Internet, where the whole is much greater than the sum of its parts. To get to the heart of the argument, and the heart of the choices we need to make, we therefore have to lift our view to the system as a whole.

The Network Architecture Argument

The reason we are implementing Open Access today is that our information and communications architecture has profoundly changed. The Internet and the web have radically increased the number of people any given person can reach, and have reduced the costs of information transfer. In both cases the changes are by orders of magnitude. And with those changes possibilities are now in reach that simply weren't before.

Let us consider a very simple model of information diffusion. The probability that information reaches a person who will make use of it can be thought of as a function of three parameters. The first of these is the total number who would be interested, i.e., the number who would in an ideal world use it were they to have access. The second parameter is the proportion of those interested people who are able to find the research in the first place, i.e. the reach of your communication tools. Multiplying these two numbers together (the fraction that can use it times the fraction that can find it) gives you the proportion that could use the information. But we also need to divide this number by a third parameter—the friction, which represents the difficulty in using the information once you have it. The full calculation (see Box 2) then allows us to determine the proportion of people that actually do use it.

Box 2. Proportions of Re-use

We can express this network model with a simplified equation that gives the proportion (or probability) of re-use:

$$P = \frac{I \bullet R}{F}$$

Where: P is the probability of information reaching a place where it can be used, or of a contribution being made to a project; I is the overall interest, the proportion of the population that could use the information, or could contribute; R is the reach of the

---

communication method; and F is the friction to use, meaning how hard it is to use the information or to contribute.

The equation is an illustration—it oversimplifies a wide range of issues but is useful for seeing how even when something is difficult to use, such as raw medical literature, if there is a wide interest then by simply making it accessible the impact is significantly enhanced. It is interesting to consider what the units of the various terms might be and whether some, particularly the friction term, should have an exponent. A fully worked model would also need to include multi-step and non-linear transmission of resources to their ultimate site of application. This could likely be treated as a Hidden Markov model [11] or as a dynamic Bayesian network [12]. A full information theoretic analysis of the system is left as an exercise for the informed reader.

Let's imagine that for some piece of information the level of interest is one in a million. If the information can reach the entire world then there are about 7,000 people who could potentially use this information. As long as people can find the information easily and the friction to use it is sufficiently low, we can be confident of this work being used. On the other hand if we don't communicate effectively or if we make it difficult to use the information, it is easy to imagine that the user base would diminish rapidly.

Until 20–30 years ago the number of people we could reach was limited by the costs and logistics of print distribution. This meant that targeting was critical; finding that right few thousand people was the main focus. If targeting them increased friction for others (like paywalls) then that was a reasonable price to pay to ensure that the people we knew were most interested had the information brought to their attention.

The underlying promise of the web is that this concept is upended. The Internet, the web, and finally the read-write web have changed the number of people who can be reached from a few hundred or a few thousand to millions or even billions. With these numbers it can now be more efficient to take a scattergun approach; to reach the maximum number of people and reduce friction for all of them rather than to focus simply on targeting a few.

This is the effect that drives successful crowdsourcing, which is destroying the business model of newspapers, and which has lead to the proliferation of online communities. The level of interest in counting insects, selling through classified ads, or talking about some element of pop culture hasn't changed, but the friction has decreased—clicking a browser button is easier than joining an ecological society or getting a PhD—and the reach has increased across a threshold level that changes the nature of the system. Many of the most successful citizen science efforts gained critical mass because the story was picked up and transmitted by mainstream media—reaching beyond the community of those already engaged in a specific scientific effort.

These shifts and changes are analogous to transitions that occur in simple networks and are easy to simulate. As the connectivity of a network increases, there is a sharp transition that occurs from a state where there are disconnected clusters to one in which most nodes are connected and a single network spans the whole system. In simple networks such as those shown in Figure 1, these transitions are highly predictable, and they occur when the probability of each point being connected (or conversely the friction) reaches a specific value. These are "disorder to order" phase transitions, similar to the crystallisation of a solid from a solution. And like physical phase transitions, they occur under predictable conditions, despite the fact that the individual components of the system behave in an unpredictable fashion.

Figure 1. Simulations of a simple percolation network.

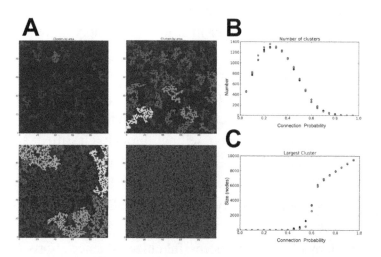

A 100×100 matrix was created with each position on the lattice being given a random number between zero and one. To simulate a simple percolation network [13] with increasing connectivity a threshold value was raised in increments of 0.05 from zero to one. When the value at a given position was lower than the threshold value the position was considered connected to the four positions around it. The threshold value is therefore the probability of connection (or the inverse of friction). (A) Four coloured plots show the size and shape of clusters at different threshold values (0.4, 0.5, 0.6, 0.8) where the cluster is coloured by its size. (B) The total number of clusters for three independent simulations. The plot shows an increase in the number of small clusters to a certain level after which the number of clusters drop as they start to connect. Overall behaviour is similar between three independent simulations. (C) The size of the largest cluster in the model. Up to a specific connection probability the simulation is dominated by many small clusters. At a specific probability a rapid change in size is observed as the majority of clusters connect. Behaviour is highly consistent across three independent simulations. The code used to generate the figures is available at: https://gist.github.com/cameronneylon/6033364.doi:10.1371/journal.pbio.1001691.g001

Clearly we do not live, or do science, on a simple square lattice. Yet many of the success stories of Open Research approaches and widening access seem to have some similar characteristics. In successes from the Polymath project [2],[3] to Galaxy Zoo [4], and from successful Open Source projects to Craigslist [5], a combination of scale and ease of use are the key to the story. It is also possible to look at failed efforts in crowd-funding, and in citizen science and crowdsourcing and see similar patterns. The reasons behind a lack of success can usually be traced to a failure to reach sufficient scale, which is often in turn associated with too much friction, preventing easy user interaction.

The "proportion of reuse" equation proposed in Box 2 is at best an analogy. These simple networks however show more promise as the beginnings of a model. They can provide an approach to identifying system parameters that are important in determining the system behaviour. They can provide a test-bed where we can make comparisons with what we observe in our real research environment and a place where we can run experiments that we couldn't do in the real world. Models can serve different functions in the physical and the social sciences. In the former they provide quantitative predictions and a mental framework that is intended to mirror the true behaviour of the system. In the latter, models are more a mode of working, a means of suggesting where to look for interesting behaviour, without necessarily being expected to define an underlying truth.

The simple models shown here cannot yet have the status of a quantitative model. Nor are they predictive. They do however provide a means of understanding specific events. The successes in Open Approaches, such as Galaxy Zoo, occur because they are close enough to a transition to take advantage of it. In many cases this may have been in large part due to luck. But this does not need to be the case. If these network models are currently only interpretative, then our aspiration must surely be to make them sophisticated enough to obtain sufficient real world data and to make them predictive.

If we accept the idea that these transitions exist then the question we must ask ourselves is how do we build an architecture that makes them as large as possible, and how do we identify how to move towards them. In a world of limited resources where we have to make choices what is the best way to maximise the number of potential users and reduce friction? To make such choices we need data and we need frameworks for decision-making built on models with predictive and analytical power.

The Financial Argument

The question of resources brings us to a core issue. If we are obliged to make choices about how we communicate research—if we must choose exactly what friction to reduce, and what people we will commit resources to reach—then it follows that we ought to make that choice wisely. There may be a tension between reaching more people and the financial costs that this incurs.

For Open Access to articles at least it turns out this isn't the case. Open Access provided by new publishers is cheaper than traditional subscription publishing [6],[7] and also enables research findings to reach more people, thereby facilitating their re-use. Making research available through repositories can also deliver greatly enhanced access with limited additional costs [7]. There are transitional costs involved in the shift to Open Access, particularly the issues of paying twice as revenue streams shift from subscriptions to other channels. But through careful management and a balance between the repository and journal routes the transitional costs can be minimised and massive potential downstream savings released [6],[7]. If, and it is admittedly a big if, we can transition via a blend of repository and journal based Open Access to an effective market in publication services then the transitional costs can be effectively constrained. If we get it right then we can also bring the long-term savings forward and use them to support more effective sharing.

The cost benefits that we can realise for Open Access articles depend in large part on an existing funded infrastructure, an existing platform for transmitting and managing these resources. But if the network argument made above holds for articles then it necessarily also applies to other kinds of research output, particularly data, but also materials.

It is interesting that some of the strongest evidence we have for the benefits of open approaches are for data, specifically the data from the human genome project where the economic returns from the publicly shared genome project were significantly greater than those from the competing closed project [8]. This success relied on an investment in the infrastructure for sharing DNA sequences, an infrastructure that is now a core part of modern biological research.

But for some other data types the platforms have yet to be created or are currently under funded. In terms of materials, platforms only exist for the sharing of very specific types.

Building the right kinds of platform can increase reach, and reduce friction, but it also requires investment. The distinction between data sharing and material sharing is also not as great as it seems. And in a world where it can be cheaper to re-do an analysis than to store the data, we need to consider seriously the social, physical, and material infrastructure that might support the sharing of the material outputs of research.

Global large scale data and materials sharing is almost certainly too expensive to consider today, but we should work hard to identify the places where it can bring the greatest benefits. There will be arguments around public access, network architecture, and cost to balance and consider but with limited resources we cannot tackle the whole space immediately. But as we reap the benefit of the transition to Open Access we need to consider, as a community, where we can best apply the billions of dollars that we will liberate from subscription budgets. The key question will be how to gather the information and build the models that will help us make those choices at the system level. Without better data on how research outputs are being used we will be flying blind, but obtaining better data will also require investment.

Mapping The Future - Foundations And Architecture

If the opportunities that we have today to re-think and mould the architecture of our communication and sharing systems are huge, then the challenges are also significant. Resources for research will continue to be flat or falling for the foreseeable future as the global economy stutters towards recovery. We will need to make difficult choices on resource allocation, and particularly to understand the balance between supporting the research itself and its communication.

These choices are not about which projects to fund or which infrastructure to build. We are bad at picking winners and show no signs of getting any better. The choices we should make are rather about how to configure the systems, how to design the processes by which we make choices, so as to optimise the overall outcome. But at the moment we have neither the models to help us do this design work, nor the data to test such models.

It is not simply, as Jeff Hammerbacher once pithily stated that "The best minds of my generation are thinking about how to make people click ads" [9]. Those "best minds" also have much better data on information flow and usage than we have in the research community. The data we have are poor and expensive, the analytics limited at best. Compare the sophistication that free tools such as Google Analytics provide in dissecting how well an advertisement with two subtly different borders performs with our ability to understand whether citations refer to the argument in a paper or the use of its data.

We have choices ahead of us, as well as opportunities to deliver significant changes in our research capacity. If we get them right. To make the right choices we need both the frameworks to help us understand the complex systems of research communication and much more data to test and utilise those frameworks. We don't just need infrastructures for sharing content and data. We need infrastructures that support the sharing of data about the sharing process.

Ultimately, while sharing knowledge more effectively is generally a greater public good in its own right, in the longer term it may be that significant benefits arise from our increased ability to understand how effectively that knowledge is being shared. The closed systems of the past were a necessary balance between reach, targeting, and resources. The tensions between these key issues today are entirely different to what they were in a print world. But we don't yet understand in detail how. Developing that understanding is critical to realise the full benefits of Open Access and Open Data in a resource limited world.

References

1. Joseph H (2013) The open access movement grows up: taking stock of a revolution. PLOS Biol 11 (10) e1001686 doi: 10.1371/journal.pbio.1001686. View Article PubMed/NCBI Google Scholar

2. Gowers T (2009) Is massively collaborative mathematics possible? Gowers's Weblog. Available: http://gowers.wordpress.com/2009/01/27/is-massively-collaborative-mathematics-possible/. Accessed 9 August 2013.

3. Nielsen M (2013) Polymath1Wiki. Available: http://michaelnielsen.org/polymath1/index.php?title=Main_Page. Accessed 9 August 2013.

4. Galaxy Zoo (n.d.) Available: http://www.galaxyzoo.org/. Accessed 9 August 2013.

5. About, Craigslist (n.d.) Available: http://www.craigslist.org/about/sites. Accessed 9 August 2013.

6. CEPA LLP, Mark Ware Consulting Ltd. (2011) Heading for the open road: costs and benefits of transitions in scholarly communications | Report Commissioned by the RIN, Research Libraries UK, the Wellcome Trust, the Publishing

Research Consortium and the Joint Information Systems Committee. Available: http://www.rin.ac.uk/ur-work/ communicating-and-disseminating-research/heading-open-road-costs-and-benefits-transitions-s. Accessed 23 December 2011.

7. Swan A, Houghton J (2012) Going for Gold? The costs and benefits of Gold Open Access for UK research institutions: further economic modelling. Report to the UK Open Access Implementation Group. Available: http://repository.jisc.ac.uk/ id/eprint/610. Accessed 16 September 2013

8. Tripp M, Grueber M (2011) Economic impact of the human genome project, Battelle Memorial Institute Report. Available: http://battelle.org/docs/default-document-library/ economic_impact_of_the_human_genome_project.pdf. Accessed 16 September 2013

9. Vance A (2011) This tech bubble is different, Bloomberg Businessweek Magazine. Available: http:// www.businessweek.com/magazine/content/11_17/ b4225060960537.htm. Accessed 16 September 2013

10. Houghton J, Swan A (2011) Access to research and technical information in Denmark. Available: http://eprints.soton.ac.uk/ 272603/. Accessed 16 September 2013

11. Hidden Markov Model, Wikipedia. Available: http:// en.wikipedia.org/wiki/Hidden_Markov_model. Accessed 16 September 2013

12. Dynamic Bayesian Network, Wikipedia. Available: http://en.wikipedia.org/wiki/Dynamic_Bayesian_network. Accessed 16 September 2013

13. Percolation theory, Wikipedia. Available: http://en.wikipedia.org/wiki/Percolation_theory Accessed 16 September 2013

Cameron Neylon is Advocacy Director for the Public Library of Science, a research biophysicist and well known agitator for opening up the process of research. He speaks regularly on issues of Open Science including Open Access publication, Open Data, and Open Source as well as the wider technical and social issues of applying the opportunities the internet brings to the practice of science. He was named as a SPARC Innovator in July 2010 for work on the Panton Principles and is a proud recipient of the Blue Obelisk for contributions to open data. He writes regularly at his blog, Science in the Open.

Facilitating Innovation: The Role Of Standards And Openness In The Broader Innovation Ecosystem

By Jochen Friedrich

Standards can play a key role in facilitating innovation. This is being taken into consideration by companies in their business strategies as well as by governments regarding their innovation strategies. Within Europe, detailed analysis has been taken regarding the complexities of the relationship between standardisation and innovation. Legal changes have been made adapting the European standardisation system to global realities in order to increase the potential in Europe for driving innovation via the powerful tool of standardisation. What is important is that the different roles which standards play in this context are well analysed and understood. Building on the boost of innovation which the internet and the world wide web produced, there is a huge potential for innovative technologies in the integration of technologies, in complex systems, in the areas that are usually tagged as "smart domains". Like with the internet and the web, standards are a critical element in these context. And flexibility and differentiated action will be required for maximising the desired effects of innovation strategies and policies.

Introduction

Innovation has been identified as a key element for flourishing economies and societies. Innovation is key for business success.

Companies everywhere, large and small, are reviewing their processes as part of their transformations towards becoming better integrated and with the objective to foster innovation in order to increase their competitiveness. And innovation is high on the political agendas around the globe. Back in 2009, European Commission President Barroso gave directions for the Commission that took office in those days: "By the end of the Commission's next mandate, I want Europe to have become not just a 'knowledge society', but an 'innovation society.' I plan to make this one of my top personal priorities. Indeed, I want it to be an important part of my legacy."[2] Since then, governments and public authorities have started or continued developing innovation policies for supporting the ongoing and necessary social and economic transformation processes. For sure, the issue of promoting innovation will continue to be an important objective for the next Commission, as well, which will get into office in 2014. An important part of both business strategies and innovation policy activities is the relationship between innovation and standardisation and the impact standards and standardisation have on innovation.

Along the lines of such strategic considerations, this paper will examine the different levels of what seems to be a complex, perhaps even sometimes conflicting, relationship between standardisation and innovation. It will look at the different roles standards play in promoting innovation.

An important aspect in this respect is openness. Standardisation is *per se* a move towards openness, towards

---

1.   José Manuel Durão Barroso, President of the European Commission, Transforming the EU into an Innovation Society, Speech at the first European Innovation Summit, Brussels, 13 October, 2009, p. 4. at:
http://europa.eu/rapid/pressReleasesAction.do?reference=SPEECH/09/478&format=HTML&aged=0&language=EN&guiLanguage=fr).

disseminating technologies and knowledge. Over the last two decades this has been complemented with trends in open innovation where businesses and governments open up their innovation processes allowing and often even inviting outside groups and communities to participate in the innovation cycles. What used to be internal and top secret has changed, has become an area for public involvement, interaction and common development. This has had its effect on standardisation, as well, most notably with the development and implementation of the concept of "Open Standards" which is part of an overall concept of "Open Platforms" and "Open Ecosystems".

Innovation Is Key, Standards Are Key Facilitators

Companies around the globe have put innovation into their focus. Innovation is critical for global competitiveness and business success. It is those companies that manage best their innovation processes and that are most ready to transform and adapt to a changing global environment which flourish and are well situated for competing on the global market.

Almost a decade ago, IBM undertook a survey amongst global CEOs on innovation.[3] For this survey interviews were held with "765 CEOs, business executives and public sector leaders from around the world"[4]. The title of the study, "expanding the innovation horizon", is programmatic for its findings. The

---

2. Expanding the Innovation Horizon: The Global CEO Study 2006, IBM Institute for Business Value. March 2006. See http://www-935.ibm.com/services/au/bcs/html/bcs_ceostudy2006.html

4 Expanding the Innovation Horizon, p. 5.

significant changes with progressing globalisation and an increasing degree of global integration of networked economies, has over the last decade, increased the competitive pressure on companies. Therefore, new ways of working, new ways of positioning oneself, new ways of operating, new products, technologies and services etc. need to be found, need to be developed. And they can be developed by actively driving the transformation of becoming a business that is fit to play within the changing and challenging global ecosystem. Yet, what is needed for making the transformation successful is constant innovation on all levels:

"Business model innovation matters. Competitive pressures have pushed business model innovation much higher than expected on CEOs' priority lists. But its importance does not negate the need to focus on products, services and markets, as well as operational innovation."[5]

In other words, innovation is not a single task of getting new technologies out, new, cool features implemented in products. It is much more: it is looking at all levels of operation. And it is above all in the integration of technologies to achieve an optimisation of processes, increase knowledge about the interrelation of processes and tasks, and about providing added value on top of already implemented structures and processes. This is what is behind "smart" or "intelligent" solutions. Smart city, smart grid, intelligent water management, intelligent transport systems – what this actually means is to be innovative by transforming existing processes adding layers and elements of intelligence in order to optimise, gain efficiency, reduce waste.

Standardisation plays a key role in these transformation processes promoting and enabling innovation on the various levels

---

5   Expanding the Innovation Horizon, p. 4.

and especially regarding the integration of technologies. By providing open information about formats, protocols, APIs, etc. standards allow the combination of technologies and the incremental addition of new, innovative technology modules into existing architectures, e.g. under the paradigm of service oriented architectures (SOA) or with a perspective of cloud technologies also with respect to Software as a Service (SaaS), Infrastructure as a Service (IaaS) or Platform as a Service (PaaS) etc.

Cloud technologies as such strongly rely on open standards and the integration of technologies. Standards provide a trusted base for the use and implementation of technologies, enable and ensure interoperability and portability, prevent vendor lock-in and ensure implementability in open source:

"[...] if moving to the cloud locks the organization to a particular cloud service provider, the organization will be at the mercy of the service level and pricing policies of that provider. With that in mind, portability and interoperability become crucial to providing the freedom to work with multiple cloud providers.

"Interoperability is concerned with the ability of systems to communicate. In the world of cloud computing, this means the ability to write code that works with more than one cloud provider simultaneously, regardless of the differences between the providers. On the other hand, portability is the ability to run components or systems written for one environment in another environment."[6]

In this respect, standards fulfil a critical function regarding the acceptability and adoption of new and innovative technologies like the Cloud. Companies, acting as customers, see these aspects

---

6 Moving to the Cloud: A white paper produced by the Cloud Computing Use Cases Discussion Group, Version 1.0, 28 February 2011, pp. 7-8 (Available at http://www.cloudstandardscustomercouncil.org/whitepaper-movingtothecloud.htm).

and therefore request the use of standards. This increases choice and flexibility – and leaves room for new innovative offerings to be taken up more rapidly and without high exit costs at any given point in time in the future. In the same way the use of standards triggers innovation because technology and service providers have an opportunity to offer and provide innovative new technologies to any customer due to the ability to integrate these solutions with reduced efforts due to the use of standards based infrastructures.

Innovation At The Core Of EU Standards Policy

On the political level in Europe the relation between standardisation and innovation and the positive effects of standards for promoting innovation have been analysed and addressed by the European Commission, the Council and the European Parliament at various instances and with some special focus since the mid of the last decade.[7] As a result, the topic of standardisation has been raised at prominent level in the various flagship initiatives of the current Commission and has become part of the Commission's Europe 2020 strategy. So, for example, the Innovation Union Flagship Initiative clearly states: "Standards play an important role for innovation. By codifying information on the state of the art of a particular technology, they enable dissemination of knowledge, interoperability between new

---

7 A little overview of the discussion up until mid 2008 is given in: Towards an increased contribution from standardisation to innovation in Europe, Communication from the European Commission to the European Parliament, the Council, the European Economic and Social Committee and the Committee of the Regions, COM(2008) 133, pp. 1-2 (Available at http://eur-lex.europa.eu/ LexUriServ/LexUriServ.do?uri=COM:2008:0133:FIN:en:PDF).

products and services and provide a platform for further innovation."[8] Not only does that stress the importance of standards in relation to innovation and innovation policy, it also indicates a number of different effects standards may have: codifying state-of-the-art, disseminating knowledge, facilitating interoperability and providing a platform for further innovation. This builds on what the Commission had explicit addressed in the Communication on Standardisation and Innovation from 2008:

"dynamic standardisation is an important enabler of innovation. This occurs in different ways:

(a)Standards that express the state of the art give innovators a level playing field facilitating interoperability and competition between new and already existing products, services and processes. Standards provide customers with trust in the safety and performance of new products and allow differentiation of products through reference to standardised methods;

(b)The development of new standards is also necessary to accompany the emergence of new markets and the introduction of complex systems, such as the expansion of the Internet;

(c)The use of standards contributes to diffusing knowledge and facilitating the application of technology; this may then trigger innovation, in particular non-technological innovation in the service sector."[9]

---

8   Europe 2020 Flagship Initiative Innovation Union, Communication from the European Commission to the European Parliament, the Council, the European Economic and Social Committee and the Committee of the Regions, COM(2010) 546, p. 16 (Available at http://ec.europa.eu/research/innovation-union/pdf/innovation-union-communication_en.pdf#view=fit&pagemode=none).

9   Towards an increased contribution from standardisation to innovation in Europe, p. 3.

This analysis, among other aspects, differentiates between the use of standards on the one hand and the development of standards on the other. Or, in other words, the codifying and dissemination of knowledge and technologies on the one hand and the use, implementation and platform-creation on the other hand.

Looking at Information and Communication Technologies (ICT) the Commission addressed the relation of standards and innovation in much detail, most notably in the Digital Agenda for Europe (DAE)[10] and in the Communication on European Standardisation.[11] The special role of global ICT technologies is also recognised in the Regulation on European Standardisation (1025/2012).[12] Acknowledging positive effects of ICT standards for innovation the Commission has looked at the framework conditions for making these standards available for use and implementation in EU policies and in public procurement. While the European standardisation system is built on the three formally recognised European Standards Organisations (ESOs) CEN, CENELEC and ETSI, a large number of the most relevant global

---

10 A Digital Agenda for Europe: Communication from the European Commission to the European Parliament, the Council, the European Economic and Social Committee and the Committee of the Regions, COM(2009) 245 (Available at http://eur-lex.europa.eu/LexUriServ/LexUriServ.do?uri=CELEX: 52010DC0245R%2801%29:EN:NOT).

11 A strategic vision for European standards: Moving forward to enhance and accelerate the sustainable growth of the European economy by 2020, Communication from the European Commission to the European Parliament, the Council, the European Economic and Social Committee and the Committee of the Regions, COM(2011) 311 (Available at http://eur-lex.europa.eu/ LexUriServ/LexUriServ.do?uri=COM:2011:0311:FIN:EN:PDF)

12 Regulation of the European Parliament and of the Council on European Standardisation, 1025/2012 (Available at http://eur-lex.europa.eu/LexUriServ/ LexUriServ.do?uri=OJ:L:2012:316:0012:0033:EN:PDF).

standards and specifications in ICT is developed in global fora and consortia like W3C, OASIS or the IETF. The Commission identified the issue that the standards and specifications from such organisations have not been available for direct referencing in EU policies and public procurement. The Regulation contains a process to complement the European standardisation system by identifying standards and specifications from fora and consortia so that they can be used in public procurement, provided that they meet a distinct set of criteria listed in Annex II of the Regulation. These criteria include openness, transparency, balance, etc. In effect, this new process forms a necessary basis for a more effective innovation policy and for improved conditions in public procurement. It is, as it were, a precondition for the overall direction for policy making in Europe in the area of ICT:

"Europe does not yet reap the maximum benefit from interoperability. Weaknesses in standard-setting, public procurement and coordination between public authorities prevent digital services and devices used by Europeans from working together as well as they should. The Digital Agenda can only take off if its different parts and applications are interoperable and based on standards and open platforms."[13]

Following this analysis from the Digital Agenda the Commission explicitly stresses the need of global standards and specifications from fora and consortia in the context of innovation policy in the Communication "A strategic vision for European standards" - not in conflict, but complementary to European standards developed by the ESOs:

> "In the new global era, the policy role of standardisation process cannot be limited to supporting European legislation. Today, standardisation is

---

13   Digital Agenda, p. 5.

increasingly happening at global level in many areas, often, like in the field of ICT, through dynamic and fast-paced fora and consortia. In this context, the strategic use of standards on the one hand and European standardisation on the other, are strategic assets for securing EU competitiveness and a key tool for knowledge dissemination, interoperability, validation of novel ideas and promotion of innovation. "[14]

In summary, the European Commission has developed a rather holistic view on the relation of standardisation and innovation. This ranges from the analysis of the interrelationship and of the roles standards play in supporting innovation to the concrete proposals for legal changes so that the European standardisation system is better suited to support policy makers as well as all stakeholders regarding innovation processes and policies. This has been done in close cooperation with the Council. Moreover, the new Regulation also accommodates some of the requirements voiced by the European Parliament already in its 2010 report on the Future of European Standardisation – namely that the revision of the European standardisation system must contribute to innovation and that for ICT specific changes are required for making global ICT standards and specifications available for implementation and use in EU policies and public procurement.[15] The actions taken and the legal proposals provided by the Commission are intended to support the creation of an innovation-

---

14   A strategic vision for European standards, p. 4.

15   European Parliament resolution of 21 October 2010 on the future of European standardisation (2010/2051(INI)), recommendations 3-8 (Available at http://www.europarl.europa.eu/sides/getDoc.do?type=TA&reference=P7-TA-2010-0384&language=EN).

friendly ecosystem in Europe and putting the European public sector on the forefront.

In addition, with the implementation of the EU ICT Multi-Stakeholder Platform (MSP) as the central advisory body to the European Commission on all matters relating ICT standardisation the Commission ensures a high level of information exchange and information flow.[16] All major stakeholders in European ICT standardisation are part of the MSP. This has global impact on driving new topic areas that are relevant for innovation and growth and where ICT standards play in role in supporting innovation policy. On the level of detailed planning the Commission works closely with the MSP on developing the EU Rolling Plan for ICT Standardisation which contains all major areas of activity including a listing of ongoing work on the global level and of concreted actions.[17]

Basic Levels Regarding The Role Of Standards In Relation To Innovation

There is no such thing like one stringent causation on how standards promote innovation. Much rather, standards can have different positive effects promoting innovation in different contexts. It is an inter-relation with some level of complexity, depending on the technology domain and on the role which standards play. Therefore, there may well be different

---

16   Decision 2011/C 349/04 of the European Commission: http://ec.europa.eu/transparency/regexpert/index.cfm?do=groupDetail.groupDetail&groupID=2758

17   EU Rolling Plan on ICT Standardisation: http://ec.europa.eu/enterprise/sectors/ict/standards/work-programme/index_en.htm

requirements for an effective innovation policy which intends to leverage the positive effects of standardisation.

Standards are a vital tool for disseminating new technologies: For bringing a new, innovative technology to the market, preferably the global market, standards are a key facilitator. They make technologies available and promote their uptake. This has always been one of the elementary benefits of standards. Standardisation in this sense is the "second step" to market success complementing the innovation process in base technology and product development. Standardisation here is a tool based on a clear business decision to achieve business success on the global market. This can also be very effective for the transfer of research results into innovative new products and offerings on the market.

Standards facilitate market access in regulatory domains: Standards are an effective tool for complying with regulatory requirements and thus for enabling access to markets. This concerns for instance the areas of health and safety where governments have specific requirements that need to be met by standards. Ideally, and in accordance with the WTO TBT Agreement, global standards should be applied and regional or national barriers to trade need to be avoided. This promotes innovations on a global scale and for global markets. And it allows a fast and unencumbered access of innovative technologies and offerings globally.

Standards ensure interoperability: By openly describing interfaces, protocols, formats, etc. standards provide all necessary information for accessing coded content and for connecting technologies. Interoperability is a critical element of modern, state-of-the-art, open ICT architectures and infrastructures. Interoperability allows for a modular infrastructure design and is at the core of Service Oriented Architectures (SOA). It increases flexibility and choice, helps to avoid lock-in and reduces exit cost for technologies. In this respect, standards and interoperability open the way for innovative products and technologies to be offered in competitive situations where replacement of older or less innovative technologies can fairly easily be done. Lock-in situations are avoided and vendors have a fair and equal chance for competing.

Standard provide a trusted and solid technology base for innovation to take place on the level of the implementation of standards: Given the benefits of interoperability and the opportunities for competing with other vendors standards encourage innovators to develop new, innovative products and offerings while implementing the respective standard. This means the differentiation with other vendors' products and offerings takes place on the level of the implementation. The standard, however, ensures that the innovations can be brought to the marketplace.

Standards facilitate the integration of technologies into innovative systems: A large potential for innovation today is in the integration of processes and technologies which is made possible via combining different standards. This applies to many areas and sectors. For example, companies increase their level of process integration and of automatic processing of data and transactions. Similarly, communication between parties is integrated – on all levels, be it B2B, B2C, A2A, A2B, A2C etc. Moreover, systems and processes can be optimised via the innovative integration of technologies. This can be seen in almost all areas and sectors, be it eGovernment, eHealth, smart grid, intelligent transportation, eMobility etc. Where ICT are used to optimise things and create smarter systems standards play a key role as enabler of such innovation.

Standards allow access to coded information for innovative add-on solutions: Not only the integration of technologies is important for creating innovative, smart solutions, but also the ability to make use of information that is coded so that this information can be analysed and optimisation choices can be made. Standards ensure open access to such information by providing descriptions of the respective data structures, formats, protocols, APIs, etc. This makes it possible for innovators to develop new technologies that, for instance, add a new level of intelligent layer providing added-value for systems management and for smarter ways of optimising and doing the things that are done. Again, examples are manifold, be it smart water supply, smart home, smart cities, or the vast field of public sector information (PSI) where public data available in open formats based on standards is used in highly innovative ways leading to new insight and improvements and providing a base for new businesses and growth.

Strategic Considerations Regarding The Relation Of Standardisation And Innovation

Any strategy regarding standardisation and innovation will take these different roles standards play in enabling innovation into account. And policy makers will look at means how they can best provide the framework for allowing a differentiated approach towards exploiting the full potential of standards in the context of innovation policy. A key criterion here is the analysis where the "innovative act" takes place and what its relation is towards the standard.

As we have seen standards can play a key role in disseminating technologies and bringing innovations to the marketplace. The innovative act happened first, way before the standardisation activity, with the development or invention of new technologies or techniques. The transfer of technologies into standardisation usually takes place on the basis of a clear business case. Considerations in this context include whether the opening up of technologies in the process of standardisation will allow for some rewarding of the research activities and efforts spent on developing and inventing the new technologies. The market has developed a patent system and a patent licensing system. Standards bodies have implemented policies on how intellectual property rights (IPR) are handled. Licensing on "Fair, Reasonable And Non-Discriminatory" (FRAND) terms and conditions is the common practice which has also been accepted by public authorities as a minimum framework condition for standards to be supplied and used in policies and public procurement in general.

On the other hand, standards can play a key role in providing a platform, a common, agreed basis on which innovation can take place. Examples we discussed are innovation on the level of the implementation of a standard, integration of technologies, access to coded information, etc. In such instances the innovative act takes place using the standards that are available and implemented while interoperability ensured by standards is the key driver for such innovations. In other words, this is not about turning inventions, innovative technologies into a standard, it is about using a standard for developing innovative techniques, technologies and solutions.

What is highly relevant here is the unencumbered availability and broad adoption of the standard. This is where Open Standards play an important role. There are different levels of openness and a number of different definitions exist about what constitutes an

"Open Standard".[18] Most violently the debate has been held on the requirements regarding licensing terms and conditions and to what extend a standard that is available under FRAND terms and conditions is actually an Open Standard. It is fair to say, however, that the more common usage of the term Open Standard implies that IPRs in the standard are available Royalty-free. In this sense the term Open Standard had been used in the European Interoperability Framework and had been adopted by several governments in Europe and around the globe.

The Role Of Open Standards In Enabling Software Interoperability And Driving Innovation

Over the last 10 to 15 years openness has become the leading paradigm for economies and societies. And innovation that builds on openness can be seen on all levels – the public sphere as well as in business. Crowd sourcing and community-based work have become common ways introducing open innovation mechanisms which complement the traditional structures in industry. A new equilibrium between proprietary and open has established and is challenging companies of all sectors and in all geographies. The concept of Open Standards can be seen as an integral part in this overall trend and move.

Open Standards play a critical role in software interoperability. They have major benefits in this context: (i) Open Standards are available for everyone for free, without encumbrances on their use and implementation. This way they

---

18   For a first and rough overview see the Wikipedia entry on Open Standard: http://en.wikipedia.org/wiki/Open_standard.

promote interoperability on the broad scale and ensure that technologies can be integrated, innovative new products and technologies can be added into open architectures and platforms, etc. And (ii), Open Standards can be implemented in open source and therefore allow for a level playing field regarding proprietary versus open source offerings. Open Standards are also essential if open source technologies are to be combined and integrated into infrastructures.

Open Standards for software interoperability have rightly been made a requirement by a number of countries and public administrations. Open Standards ensure open platforms where also open source communities can contribute. Similarly open data that is available in formats based on Open Standards can be used and exploited by everyone without constraints and to the benefit of the public.

The prime example for how Open Standards can boost innovation are the internet and the world wide web. These Open Standards, developed within then new platforms like the Internet Engineering Task Force (IETF) and the World Wide Web Consortium (W3C) have been available for free for everyone to use and implement. With the standards like TCP/IP, http, html etc. and the establishment of the world wide web there was a base available, agreed and globally implemented, which enabled and fostered innovation in an unprecedented way. The standards guarantee connectivity and interoperability in an open infrastructure. No constraints, no royalty fees to pay. This has become an open road for innovation. And a major driver for growth – both on the global scale but also regarding the many small and medium sized enterprises everywhere that prosper because of the internet and because of implementing the standards. Included are web hosting shops, web design shops, web shops themselves, etc. Open Standards are at the core of this.

They promoted the biggest boost in innovation we have seen in the last decades.

What can be seen today is that for this decade up until 2020 an enormous potential for innovation lies in the integration of technologies. And ICT technologies are at the core of these innovations.

The integration of technologies and the use of ICT in complex systems is paramount in the context of solutions for a smarter planet. Innovation here is already taking place by delivering intelligent infrastructures that are highly efficient and overlay the physical infrastructure with digital intelligence. Innovations occur in the development of intelligent systems that use open standards to provide near real-time information for more efficient management of the infrastructure, e.g. in the context of water quantities, or, even, entire transportation systems. Smart metering or smart Grid is another example here. And for sure the Cloud is taking a leading role in driving innovation and further transforming economies and societies.

Further Building And Strengthening An Innovation-Friendly Ecosystem

The European Commission has largely addressed the issue of innovation and the role standards play as an enabler for innovative technologies. Openness and Information and Communication Technologies (ICT) are major drivers in this respect. As President Barroso had outlined, "the application of innovations like Web 2.0 to business and public life is changing the way in which innovation happens. It is becoming more open and collaborative. Once the preserve of a select elite, it now involves a much wider range of actors. [...] crowd-sourcing and co-creation are now the order of the day! We need a new policy that reflects these changes. This means that we will have to, well, innovate!"[19] The Digital Agenda has driven the European priorities in this respect with a number of focussed action items and areas that are being addressed. The new Commission coming into place in 2014 will certainly continue along this successful path.

The Commission follows a holistic approach with an analysis of the complexities in the relation between standardisation and innovation and with a legal proposal to adapt the basic structure of European standardisation to global trends and realities especially in the ICT sector. This will further strengthen the potential of standardisation in Europe to facilitate and even drive innovation.

On the further level of implementation a differentiated approach towards standardisation and innovation is required. The different roles standards can play in promoting innovation need to be taken into consideration both in business strategies and on the policy level in innovation and industrial policy. In this respect, industry should continue working with a clear commitment to standards and standardisation. This includes a commitment to contribute to standardisation, take technical leadership in standards bodies and to be willing to license technologies so that they can be used in standardisation. At any rate, the process of transformation for coping in the new paradigm of openness will continue, if not increase in intensity, and industry will further be challenged to find a new balance between proprietary and open.

Public authorities can make use of their powers by putting a strong focus on the potential for innovation that lies in the integration of technologies and standards. Also, public authorities should more stringently reference standards in public

---

[19] Barroso, President of the European Commission, Transforming the EU into an Innovation Society, p. 4.

procurement. Open Standards should explicitly be required in public policies and in procurement where software interoperability is concerned.

Finally, standardisation needs strong and vital platforms, the standards bodies. They also need to move on with providing a flexible environment that is able to support innovation in all its aspects. In particular they need to be able to support the different roles standards can play in enabling and driving innovation. This might require the implementation of more dynamic or flexible rules and structures. Standards bodies will need to look whether the policies and processes in place are suitable also for open innovation in standards development. And they should be open to learn from each other – including best practices as applied in global fora and consortia.

Standards are not per se a guarantee that innovation will happen. But they can be effective tool to promote and even drive innovation. This decade will see a high potential in this respect, especially where the integration of technologies and thus the combination of standards are concerned. Proper strategies for standardisation that take into account the different roles standards play in promoting innovation will be required for maximising the benefits of the complex relation between standardisation and innovation.

References

1. A Digital Agenda for Europe: Communication from the European Commission to the European Parliament, the Council, the European Economic and Social Committee and the Committee of the Regions, COM(2009) 245 (Available at http://eur-lex.europa.eu/LexUriServ/LexUriServ.do? uri=CELEX:52010DC0245R%2801%29:EN:NOT).

2. Barroso, José Manuel Durão (2009), Transforming the EU into an Innovation Society, Speech at the first European Innovation Summit, Brussels, 13 October, 2009. (Available at http://europa.eu/rapid/pressReleasesAction.do? reference=SPEECH/ 09/478&format=HTML&aged=0&language=EN&guiLangua ge=fr).

3. Decision 2011/C 349/04 of the European Commission: http:// ec.europa.eu/transparency/regexpert/index.cfm? do=groupDetail.groupDetail&groupID=2758

4. EU Rolling Plan on ICT Standardisation: http://ec.europa.eu/ enterprise/sectors/ict/standards/work-programme/ index_en.htm.

5. Europe 2020 Flagship Initiative Innovation Union, Communication from the European Commission to the European Parliament, the Council, the European Economic and Social Committee and the Committee of the Regions, COM(2010) 546 (Available at http://ec.europa.eu/research/ innovation-union/pdf/innovation-union-communication_en.pdf#view=fit&pagemode=none).

6. European Parliament resolution of 21 October 2010 on the future of European standardisation (2010/2051(INI)) (Available at http://www.europarl.europa.eu/sides/getDoc.do? type=TA&reference=P7-TA-2010-0384&language=EN).

7. Expanding the Innovation Horizon: The Global CEO Study 2006, IBM Institute for Business Value. March 2006

(Available at http://www-935.ibm.com/services/au/bcs/html/ bcs_ceostudy2006.html).

8. Moving to the Cloud: A white paper produced by the Cloud Computing Use Cases Discussion Group, Version 1.0, 28 February 2011 (Available at http:// www.cloudstandardscustomercouncil.org/whitepaper- movingtothecloud.htm).

9. Regulation of the European Parliament and of the Council on European Standardisation, 1025/2012

10. (Available at http://eur-lex.europa.eu/LexUriServ/ LexUriServ.douri=OJ:L:2012:316:0012:0033:EN:PDF).

11. Towards an increased contribution from standardisation to innovation in Europe, Communication from the European Commission to the European Parliament, the Council, the European Economic and Social Committee and the Committee of the Regions, COM(2008) 133, (Available at http://eur-lex.europa.eu/LexUriServ/LexUriServ.do? uri=COM:2008:0133:FIN:en:PDF).

12. Wikipedia, entry on Open Standard: http://en.wikipedia.org/ wiki/Open_standard.

Jochen Friedrich is a member of IBM's Technical Relations Europe team which is part of the IBM standards and open source strategy organisation. He is responsible for coordinating IBM's software standardisation activities in Europe with a special focus on telecommunications, interoperability and services as well as on open standards and the European standardisation framework.

Jochen Friedrich started his career in IBM at the Scientific Centre Heidelberg in 1998. Since then he has held several lead positions in Research and Development. He worked as operations manager for the IBM European Voice Technology Development team and was responsible for Business Development and Project Coordination for Voice Research projects in Europe. Jochen has broad experience in driving new, emerging technologies, managing multi-national and multi-company teams and setting up multi-company projects in the European Union research framework.

In addition to his IBM responsibilities, Jochen is a member of a regional board of the German Association of Electronics, Electrical Engineering and Information Technologies (VDE), he was a foundational Board member of the Enterprise Interoperability Centre (EIC) and holds lead roles in European industry associations, most notably in the OpenForum Europe (OFE) where he chairs the standardisation task force, in DigitalEurope (DE) and in the German ICT association BITKOM.

Jochen lives with his wife and two children in Heidelberg, Germany. He holds a PhD in Humanities from Heidelberg University (Germany), spent an academic year at Reading University (United Kingdom) and holds a degree as Certified Telematics Engineer.

For further information see Jochen's Open Blog (http:// jfopen.blogspot.com/) and connect with Jochen at Linked In (http://de.linkedin.com/in/jochenfriedrich).

Standards And Sustainable Infrastructures: Matching Compatibility Strategies With System Flexibility Objectives

By Tineke M. Egyedi[20]

Problems of entrenchment often severely hamper the introduction of change in large technical systems (LTSs). They lack the flexibility to innovate.

This paper explores the counter-intuitive assumption that standards increase system flexibility. To what degree and in what manner can standards—and other strategies that create technical compatibility—enhance system flexibility? It focuses on information networks of which the life cycle is sometimes needlessly short. Different objectives of system flexibility can be discerned (e.g., exchangeability and longevity). I examine to what degree specific compatibility strategies (i.e., gateway technologies, standardisation, modularity and interactive compatibility) can be matched with distinct flexibility objectives.

I conclude that compatibility is crucial to sustainable system innovation, and recommend that innovation policies should incorporate standards policy.

---

20 A version of this article was published earlier in Interoperable Nederland, Nico Westpalm van Hoorn, Peter Waters en Pieter Wisse (Eds.). Den Haag: Forum Standaardisatie, 2011, pp.379-391; and Unifier or Divider? Sherrie Bolin (Ed.), USA, Canton: Bolin Communications, Standards Edge Series, 2010, pp. 223-234.

Entrenchment

There is no discussion about the need to make large technical systems (LTSs) such as transport and energy systems more sustainable environmentally, economically, and socially. However, many LTSs seem impervious to change. This is partly due to the number, interrelatedness and interdependence of constituent socio-technical components and subsystems. LTSs comprise technical artefacts as well as institutional and regulatory elements of artefact production and use. Organizations and companies develop and sustain the system. Technical add-ons and complementary products are created. As an LTS expands, the number of and interdependencies between actors and artefacts grows. Over time, these interdependencies crystallise, solidify, and make manifest a process of socio-technical *entrenchment.*[21] To paraphrase Collingridge, changes are only possible at the expense of readjusting the technologies and other socio-technical arrangements that surround them. The larger the vested interests, the higher the costs of change.

Box 1: Entrenchment in ICT

In a large government agency, the ICT infrastructure had evolved in a piecemeal fashion. Bit by bit stand-alone, local provisions were coupled and integrated with networked functionalities. Of the 350 software systems, 150 were generic and used throughout the organisation (e.g., office software). Two hundred software systems served a special purpose and were used by specific people or only locally. Those involved identified a number of serious problems with respect to system maintenance and evolution:

- the short life cycle of IT products. IT products have a relatively short lifecycle. The average time for a software upgrade is about three years. This

---

[21] David Collingridge, *The Social Control of Technology* (Milton Keynes, UK: The Open University Press, 1981), 47.

period is close to the time needed to roll out IT products in a large organisation (i.e., from idea to working implementation). As a result, there is a continuous pressure to upgrade the infrastructure.

- different local needs. Different IT configurations at the local level (i.e., lower level of organisational unit) make it difficult to rollout IT products organisation-wide. Locally adaptations are introduced that further increases the differences between local configurations.
- unsustainable software design. Too little attention is paid to sustainable software design. For example, software developed in a certain programming environment does not automatically run in another (user) environment.
- unexpected interaction between software. New applications sometimes affect existing ones in unexpected ways.
- provider dependence. The organisation is sometimes locked into provider-dependent (closed source) software, such as off-the-shelf software of a monopolist and tailor-made software. System maintenance can become very dear.

The case illustrates that where ". . . information systems are updated, . . . frequently, the resulting system grows increasingly complex, as does the maintenance process itself . . ."[22] The complexity and further development of the ICT infrastructure become difficult to manage. The ICT system lacks the necessary flexibility.

An example of undesirable entrenchment is the production of polyvinyl chloride (PVC).[23] From the early 1930s onwards, its production posed health and environmental risks. The dangers ranged from health risks to workers and those living near

---

[22] Nancy Bogucki Duncan, "Capturing Flexibility of Information Technology Infrastructure: A Study of Resource Characteristics and
their Measure," Journal of Management Information Systems, 12, no. 2 (Fall 1995): 43.

[23] Karel Mulder and Marjolijn Knot, "PVC Plastic: A History of Systems Development and Entrenchment," Technology in Society 23, no. 2 (2001): 265-286.

production and processing plants (toxicity and carcinogenity caused by vinyl chlorine; Miamata disease due to mercury emission) to the dioxin found in cow milk as a result of incineration of PVC waste in the 1980s. Despite public protests, PVC is still produced nowadays. While the industry has improved its production, ironically this has reinforced PVC entrenchment, making the industry's conversion to non-chlorinated plastics less likely.

Apparently, such large technical systems have a *technological momentum*[24] that ". . . pushes the system along a path-dependent process of technological change . . . ".[25] Unless something radical happens, no real deviation from the set path will occur.

Theoretical concepts such as technological momentum and path-dependency suggest that significant system changes are unlikely. They reflect a deterministic view on LTS evolution and provide few clues for policy intervention. The corresponding policy dilemma, the Collingridge Dilemma, is that entrenchment problems are difficult to foresee at an early stage of technology development and are difficult to address at a later stage. Where infrastructure change is aimed for, other concepts are more promising. For example, under the heading of 'de-entrenchment strategies', Mulder and Knot propose means to recreate the critical space necessary for system change. These strategies target the system's actor network by negotiating about and redefining aspects of the critical problem (e.g., solving a different problem or

---

[24] Thomas P. Hughes, "The Evolution of Large Technological Systems," in *The Social Construction of Technological Systems: New Directions in the Sociology and History of Technology*, ed. Wiebe E. Bijker, Thomas P. Hughes, and Trevor J. Pinch (Cambridge, MA: MIT Press, 1987), 51-82.

[25] Andrew Davies, "Innovation in Large Technical Systems: The Case of Telecommunications," *Industrial and Corporate Change* 5, no. 4 (1996): 1148.

assigning a new problem owner; giving in to demands with regard to one part of the LTS in order to safeguard another; and defining the problem at a higher level in order to avoid competition within the actor network at a lower level).

In this article I focus on ways to enhance the flexibility of LTSs. Paraphrasing Feitelson and Salomon,[26] flexibility refers to the ease with which an LTS can adjust to changing circumstances and demands. It is about openness to change. Thus, a flexible design would make a system less susceptible to unwelcome, premature entrenchment. In particular, I look at standards as a means to enhance system flexibility. Certain authors note that *compatibility* or interoperability standards play a crucial role in the evolution of LTSs, but few discuss how they actually relate.

Paradox Of Standards

There is an intuitive tension between standards and flexibility.[27] Standards may foremost seem catalysts of entrenchment for two related reasons. First, standards codify existing knowledge and practices. In Reddy's wordings ". . . standardization . . . is an attempt to establish what is known,

---

[26] Eran Feitelson and Ilan Salomon, "The Implications of Differential Network Flexibility for Spatial Structures," Transportation Research Part A, 34 (2000): 463.

[27] Ole Hanseth, Eric Monteiro, and Morten Hatling, "Developing Information Infrastructure: The Tension between Standardization and Flexibility," *Science, Technologies and Human Values* 21, no. 4 (1996): 407-426.

consolidate what is common, and formalise what is agreed upon."[28] Codification is a primary source of entrenchment.

Second, the interrelatedness of multiple LTS components is a source of entrenchment as well. These components are complementarities.[29] Often, their interfaces are defined by standards. An example is the A4 paper format that specifies the interface between divers paper processing machines (e.g., copying machines, telefaxes and printers) and office requisites (e.g., folders, computer software). The standardised interface eases the entry of new market players, and increases interdependencies between actors and artefacts.[30] It stabilises the market. Entrenchment eventually befalls all useful standards.

However, a standard can also be a means to postpone system entrenchment as standardization in one part of the system creates flexibility in another[31]. Formulated differently, "interdependence among the development of complementary technologies may require the coordination provided by standardization in one

---

[28] N. M. Reddy, "Product of Self-Regulation: A Paradox of Technology Policy," *Technological Forecasting and Social Change* 38 (1990): 59.

[29] Paul A. David and Shane Greenstein, "The Economics of Compatibility Standards: An Introduction to Recent Research," *Economics of Innovation and New Technologies* 1 (1990): 7.

[30] Carl Cargill, *Information Technology Standardization: Theory, Process and Organizations* (Cambridge, MA: Digital Press, 1989); Reddy, "Product of Self-Regulation," 56.

[31] Geoff J. Mulgan, *Communication and Control: Networks and the New Economies of Communication* (New York: Guilford Press, 1990), 202.

domain so as to foster the generation of diversity in another."[32] For example, the international standard for freight container dimensions (ISO/R 668) lies at the basis of intermodal transport between sea, rail and road transport[33]. It illustrates that standards can also enhance flexibility in LTS design.

In the following the apparently paradoxical role of standards is examined more closely, whether formal standards[34], consortium or de facto standards. It is discussed in the wider context of creating local compatibility without the overall system losing the ability to evolve and innovate.

This paper is structured as follows. First, reasons to strive for system flexibility systems are discussed. Next, issues of compatibility are turned to. Different sources of compatibility and compatibility dimensions are identified. Building on the previous sections, a conceptual model is drawn up that integrates flexibility objectives and compatibility strategies, and carefully distinguish between   means and aims. The concluding section readdresses compatibility issues in the light of sustainable system evolution and innovation.

---

[32] Paul A. David, *Standardization Policies for Network Technologies: The flux between Freedom and Order Revisited* (ENCIP Working Paper Series, Montpellier, France: EEIG/ENCIP, October 1994), 25.

[33] Tineke M. Egyedi, "The Standardized Container: Gateway Technologies in Cargo Transport," in *EURAS Yearbook of Standardization*, Vol. 3 Homo Oeconomicus XVII(3), ed. Manfred Holler and Esko Niskanen (Munich: Accedo, 2000), 231-262.

[34] Formal standards are " . . . provisions for common and repeated use, aimed at the achievement of the optimum degree of order in a given context." *ISO/IEC Guide 2: General Terms and Their Definitions Concerning Standardization and Related Activities*, 1991.

Objectives Of Flexibility

Flexibility is a means and not an end in itself. Therefore, we need to know why system flexibility is sought (i.e., flexibility objectives). Many areas of technology, divers as they may be, share the same objectives.[35] For example, the automobile industry and information managers seek system flexibility to allow the introduction of changes while simultaneously preserving earlier investments. In the automobile industry, flexibility serves the purpose of creating a wider variety of personalised products, however, the general aim is the same as in others areas: to reduce engineering efforts and facilitate system maintenance. Table 1 lists some general, partly overlapping, flexibility objectives.

General Flexibility Objectives
• improvement while preserving earlier investments • reduced engineering efforts • reduced operational costs • higher system efficiency • reduced maintenance efforts • reusability

Table 1: General flexibility objectives.

---

[35] Duncan, "Capturing Flexibility of Information Technology Infrastructure"; Takahiro Fujimoto and Daniel Raff, "Conclusion," in *Coping with Variety: Flexible Productive Systems for Product Variety in the Auto Industry*, eds. Yannick Lung, J. J. Chanaron, Takahiro Fujimoto, and Daniel Raff (Aldershot, UK: Ashgate, 1999), 393-406; Feitelson and Salomon, "The Implications of Differential Network Flexibility"; Terry Anthony Byrd and Douglas E. Turner, "An Exploratory Examination of the Relationship between Flexible IT Infrastructure and Competitive Advantage" *Information and Management* 39, no. 1 (November 2001): 41-52.

Looking in more detail into flexibility requirements in ICT, reusability of system components plays a key role. It is relevant to system innovation, reengineering, and managing the rapid change of technological generations. Independent and reusable data and application components simplify ". . . processes of development, maintenance or reengineering of direct-purpose systems," and reduce their costs.[36] Reusability is an overarching aim. It comes in different shapes, and is an important element in many of the following, more specific flexibility objectives in ICT:[37]

- exchangeability, that is, exchangeable software applications, computer hardware, etc. (i.e., reuse in a different system or context, and over time),[38]

- portability, which refers to the different hardware and software platforms upon which software entities can operate and be ported (i.e., reuse on different platforms),[39]

- scalability, which refers to the possibility to use the same software on mainframe and micro-computers (i.e., reuse in smaller/larger system), [40]

---

[36] Ibid.

[37] Tineke M. Egyedi, "Standards Enhance Flexibility? Mapping Compatibility Strategies onto Flexibility Objectives" (paper presented at EASST 2002 Conference, Standardization Track, University of York, UK, July 31-August 3, 2002).

[38] J. A. Dinklo, "Open Systemen," *Informatie en Informatiebeleid* 7, no. 2 (1989): 29-36.

[39] Ibid.

[40] Ibid.

- extendibility or upgradeability (i.e., add new elements to a system in order to reuse existing parts of the system and lengthen its life-span),[41]

- integration of heterogeneous components and subsystems (i.e., reuse of part of the system by integrating new elements or by integrating different subsystems; organization internally-oriented), [42]

- interconnectivity (i.e., reuse of system through coupling with other (sub)systems; organization externally-oriented),[43]

- reversibility (i.e., reversing changes to the system), and

- downgradeability (likewise, e.g., for accessing an old archive; longevity)

Some flexibility objectives are more likely to be achieved by standards; important; for others, other means of creating compatibility may be more obvious.

---

[41] Duncan, "Capturing Flexibility of Information Technology Infrastructure."

[42] Reuse of part of a system for the purpose of integration with another system (part) is a transient form of flexibility: once integrated into a higher level system, flexibility is lost at the lower level. An example of integration can be found in Philipp Genschel, "Institutioneller Wandel in der Standardisierung van Informationstechnik" (doctoral dissertation, University of Cologne, Germany, 1993).

[43] Philipp Genschel, "Institutioneller Wandel in der Standardisierung van Informationstechnik" (doctoral dissertation, University of Cologne, Germany, 1993).

Compatibility

The term compatibility refers to the "suitability of products, processes or services for use together . . ."[44] It is used here as synonymous with 'interoperability'. As a stepping stone towards a discussion of compatibility strategies, I first address key characteristics and possible sources of compatibility.

Generic and Dedicated Gateways

The term 'compatibility' is closely related to the term 'gateway technology', which refers to " . . . a means (a device or convention) for effectuating whatever technical connections between distinct production sub-systems are required in order for them to be utilised in conjunction, within a larger integrated . . . system."[45] Gateways "make it technically feasible to utilise two or more components/ subsystems as compatible complements or compatible substitutes in an integrated system of production."[46]

Gateways differ in the scope of compatibility they achieve.[47] Some gateways are dedicated. They link an exclusive and specified number of subsystems. For example, gateways that link specific proprietary computer networks belong to this category.

---

[44] ISO/IEC, *ISO/IEC Guide, 2.*

[45] Paul A. David and Julie Ann Bunn, "The Economics of Gateway Technologies and Network Evolution: Lessons from Electricity Supply History," *Information Economics and Policy* 3, no. 2 (1988): 170.

[46] Ibid., 172.

[47] Tineke M. Egyedi, "The Standardized Container".

Other gateways have generic properties. Standards developed in committees[48] function as generic gateways. The example of the A4 paper format was mentioned earlier as an interface specification between unspecified and divers storage and processing devices. An even more generic category of standards is the reference model that guides interdependent, complementary standards activities. A well-known one in the field of ICT is the Open Systems Interconnection (OSI) Reference Model[49]. Gateway technologies can thus be categorised as dedicated, generic, or meta-generic, depending on the scope of compatibility concerned.

The degree of standardization to which a gateway is submitted, determines the scope of the gateway solution. Where no standardization has occurred, the connection between subsystems is improvised, at it were. This corresponds to a dedicated gateway. Standardized gateway solutions, which aim at connecting an unspecified number of subsystems, correspond to generic gateways. Gateways that are based on modelled (standardized) solutions, that is, standardization at the level of reference frameworks, embody meta-generic properties. SeeTable 2.

---

[48] The term "committee standardization" refers here to activities that are exclusively set up to lead to multi-party standards. They take place in formal standards bodies such as ISO, in professional organizations, and other multi-party fora (IEEE, IETF), or in standards consortia (e.g., W3C; i.e., multi-party industry standards fora).

[49] The OSI reference model (ISO 7498 and CCITT X.200) identifies logically separate generic functions in data communication. It depicts these as a set of hierarchically ordered layers, which address areas of standardization.

Level of Standardization	Scope of Gateway Solution
High (modelled)	Meta-generic
Medium (standardized)	Generic
Low (improvised)	Dedicated

Table 2: Relationship between the level of standardization
and the scope of the gateway solution.

Sources of De Facto Compatibility

The origin of de facto compatibility may differ(note: I'm *not* speaking about de facto standardization). See Table 3. The table highlights committee standardization of IT software as a multi-party specification process that leads to a standard. It is a means to coordinate the activities of competing parties.[50] Only if the standard is implemented widely does de facto compatibility result.Compare this with the compatibility achieved by de facto standards. Here, the specification process takes place in a company or in collaboration between several parties. Compatibility results as a by-product of market dominance (e.g., PDF format and Microsoft Windows).

The type of specification process need have no bearing on how ownership of the specification is handled. A company may keep the proprietary technology to itself, monopolise the

---

[50] Susanne K. Schmidt and Raymund Werle, *Coordinating Technology: Studies in the International Standardization of Telecommunication* (Cambridge, MA: MIT Press, 1998); Martin B. H. Weiss and Marvin Sirbu, "Technological Choice in Voluntary Standards Committees: An Empirical Analysis," *Economics of Innovation and New Technology* 1 (1990): 111-133.

production of a key component, and define an interface which effectively ties complementary products of other firms to the proprietary technology.[51] Or, a company or group of players may give away its technology with an eye to expected long-term advantages, or enter into coalitions with rivals to enlarge its user base and increase support for its technology. Open source software, for example, usually comes with a non-proprietary, liberal licensing regime.

Stages > Type of Specif. Process	Specification Process		Market Process	
	Participation	Outcome		
Committee Standardization	Multi-party	Standard	Implemen-ted widely?	Yes > de facto
Software Development	Multi-party (e.g., Open Source)	Specifica-tion	Market domi-nance?	compatibili-ty No > local or no
	In-company			compatib.

Table 3: Two types of specification processes may lead to de facto compatibility between software.[52]

Compatibility Dimensions

In the following, I discuss the different compatibility strategies. To my knowledge, this has not been done before. For

---

[51] David and Greenstein, "The Economics of Compatibility Standards."

[52] Source: Tineke M. Egyedi, "Strategies for de facto Compatibility: Standardization, Proprietary and Open Source Approaches to Java," *Knowledge, Technology, and Policy* 14, no. 2 (2001): 113-128.

purpose of reference, I start with dedicated gateways, which is the default strategy in most situations.

Dedicated Gateways

As defined earlier, a dedicated gateway is a device or convention that allows a limited number of subsystems to be used together. The AC/DC rotary converter, which linked the subnetworks of direct and alternating current in the early years of electricity[53] is an example, as is the Nordunet Plug[54]. This protocol provided access from different subnetworks (i.e., OSI/X. 25, EARN, DECnet, and ARPANET/IP) to a shared backbone. Both these gateways were designed to link specified subsystems.

Different views exist about the degree of flexibility which dedicated gateways provide. Hanseth emphasises the flexibility they create for experimentation at subsystem level and their importance in the phase of system building.[55]

On the other hand, these gateways work as ad hoc solutions, often worsening subsystem entrenchment. Although they may initially offer flexibility, they may turn out to be ". . . another instance of a temporary solution to the consequences of inflexibility. . . . If gateways are . . . [not standardized or modular],

---

[53] Hughes, "The Evolution of Large Technological Systems."

[54] Ole Hanseth, "Gateways—Just as Important as Standards: How the Internet Won the 'Religious War' about Standards in Scandinavia," *Knowledge, Technology, and Policy* 14, no. 3 (2001): 71-90.

[55] Ibid.

. . . they may add the sort of complexity to the infrastructure that obstructs flexibility."[56]

Standardization

As said, committee compatibility standards are generic gateway solutions. They create complements and facilitate substitution between standardized artefacts. For example, widespread use of the ISO standard for freight container dimensions created a technology—i.e., transport mode—neutral system environment. Moreover, it also created a supplier-neutral system environment (i.e., generic in the economic sense) by means of a level playing field for different vendors. Indeed, since the early days of the computer, customers have been tied to the products of their initial platform provider and have not been able to switch systems without incurring heavy costs. Dedicated interconnections between proprietary systems only partly alleviated the interoperability problem. Although technically feasible, such interconnections were too costly, numerous and cumbersome to create and sustain. In the 1980's this resulted in standards activities which focused on "open systems." Open systems are ". . . computer environments that are based on de facto or international standards, which are publicly available and supplier independent."[57]

---

[56] Duncan, "Capturing Flexibility of Information Technology Infrastructure," 49.

[57] Dinklo, "Open Systemen," 29-30.

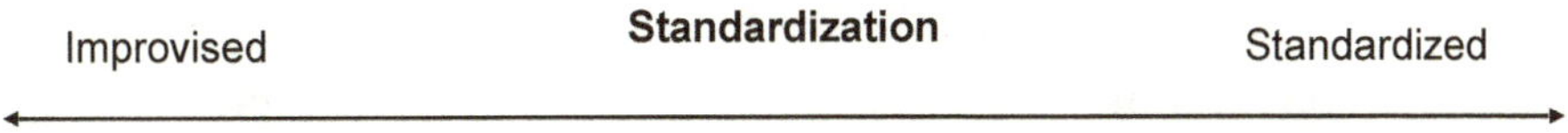

| Improvised | **Standardization** | Standardized |

Figure 2a: Standardization dimension.

Figure 2a projects degree of standardization on a dimension. Technical compatibility achieved by an ad hoc, improvised solution is portrayed to the left (i.e., no standardization). Dedicated gateways and proprietary de facto standards are categorised as such on this dimension. Highly standardized solutions such as reference models would be projected to the extreme right.

Modularity

To specify the term modularity, "A system is modular if it consists of distinct (autonomous) components, which are loosely coupled with each other, with a clear relationship between each component and its function(s) and well-defined, . . . [58] interfaces connecting the components, which require low levels of coordination."[59] In ICT modularity plays at different system

---

[58] Wolters includes "standardized interface" as a property of modularity. However, I agree with the comment of my colleague, Jos Vrancken, that "the presence of an interface is far more important than their being standardized."

[59] Matthijs J. Wolters, "The Business of Modularity and the Modularity of Business" (doctoral dissertation, Erasmus University of Rotterdam, the Netherlands, ERIM Ph.D. Series in Management no. 11, 2002).

levels. Software modules may be used in what Reitwiesner and Volkert[60] call componentware (component-based software) or, at a higher level, in pick-and-mix configurations. Modularity is the second compatibility dimension. See Figure 2d. On the left end of this dimension, the modular approach is not applied. "Improvised" solutions would be projected here (low degree of modularity). On the right end highly modular approaches are projected. The framework or reference model indicates which components or modules are included and how they are interrelated.

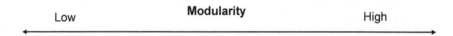

| Low | **Modularity** | High |

Figure 2b: Modularity dimension.

Interactive Compatibility

The term '(interactive) compatibility artefact' is used here to refer to technical devices and conventions that create compatibility between ICT components and (sub)systems. For example, an interface, middleware, gateways and software agents. Middleware refers to a generic building block that supports

---

[60] Bernd Reitwiesner and Stefan Volkert, "On the Impact of Standardization on the Provision of ERP-Systems as Mission Critical Business Infrastructure," in *Standards Compatibility and Infrastructure Development: Proceedings of the 6th EURAS Workshop,* eds. K. Dittrich and Tineke M. Egyedi (conference held at Delft University of Technology, Delft the Netherlands, June 28-29, 2001) 183-202.

different applications (e.g., DirectX creates 3D images in computers games; web services communicate between applications; the Java platform is used to create a vendor-independent programming environment). Gateways usually create compatibility between protocols in a fixed, static way. However, they sometimes also negotiate compatibility in a more dynamic manner. Krechmer and Baskin[61] use the term adaptability standard to capture negotiation between standardized telecommunication services: "Adaptability standards specify a negotiation process between systems which include two or more compatibility standards or variations and are used to establish communications. These standards negotiate the channel coding and/or source coding. (...) Examples include: T.30 (used with G3 facsimile), V.8, V.8bis (used with telephone modems), G.994.1 (used with DSL transceivers), and discovery protocols."

The potential relevance of negotiating compatibility also applies to non-standardized settings. In the future, agent technology may also play an important compatibility-forging role. Specific attributes of software agents are that they are autonomous, goal-driven and can negotiate and interact with their environment (i.e., can communicate, act and react on their environment.[62] These features are essential to intelligent gateways. Although the technology is still largely in the research phase, one

---

[61] Ken Krechmer and E. Baskin, "Standards, Information and Communications: A Conceptual Basis for a Mathematical Understanding of Technical Standards," in *Proceedings of the 2nd IEEE Conference on Standardization and Innovation in Information Technology*, SIIT 2001 (conference held at University of Colorado, Boulder, CO, October 3-5, 2001), 106-114.

[62] Marijn Janssen, "Designing Electronic Intermediaries: An Agent-Based Approach for Designing Interorganizational Coordination Mechanisms" (doctoral dissertation, Delft University of Technology, 2001), 11.

could imagine a future in which these agents are designed to self-organize compatibility and manage the complexity of conversion for the sake of interoperability.

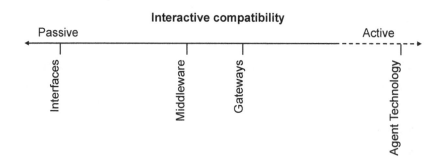

Figure 2c: Interactive compatibility dimension.

In Figure 2c, the compatibility artefacts are mapped onto the dimension of interactive compatibility. This dimension identifies artefacts as more passive or more active in forging compatibility. At the high end of this dimension, artefacts are projected that have the capacity to negotiate and interact in an intelligent and autonomous way (e.g., agent technology). At the low end, artefacts are projected that create compatibility in a passive (i.e., static and fixed) manner.

Compatibility Space

The three independent compatibility dimensions are depicted in Figure 3. The figure illustrates that each (interactive) compatibility artefact, depicted on the X-axis, can be standardized (depicted on the Y-axis) and designed in a modular way (depicted on the Z-axis). But this need not be so.

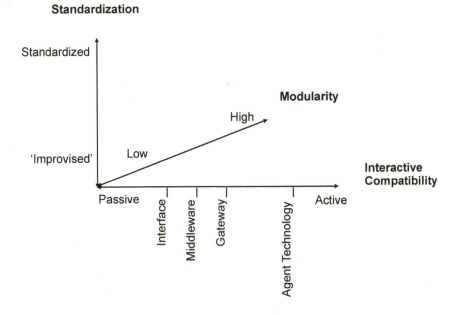

Figure 3: Three-dimensional Space of Compatibility.

The figure further draws attention to the necessity of distinguishing standardization from modularity. And most important, the figure draws attention to as yet unexplored compatibility strategies. At present most artefacts are dedicated, improvised solutions to problems of interoperability (i.e., non-standardized and non-modular). The reader is invited to reflect on a future with standardized agents and modular standards.

Each situation may need a different compatibility solution. By identifying the main dimensions, it becomes easier to discuss and prioritise compatibility solutions.

Matching Compatibility With Flexibility

Recapitulating, there are several ways to create system flexibility. Experience informs us that specific flexibility objectives are usually better achieved in certain ways than others. For example, committee standards further exchangeability; and modularity facilitates the extension and upgrading of systems.

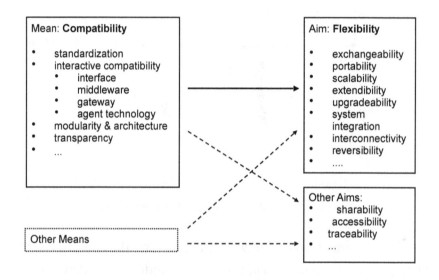

Figure 4: Elements to take into account when seeking a match between compatibility means and flexibility objectives. Although flexibility aims might be achieved by different means, the focus is here on what compatibility strategies may contribute (straight arrow).

Figure 4 models the relationship between compatibility and system flexibility as a causal one. Both categories comprise very different instances. To illustrate the model's relevance, a classic IT problem is that customers are locked-in to a specific computer platform. One solution is platform-independent computing. This would bring about system flexibility (e.g., portability and scalability). In the 1990s, the Java community developed a middleware solution to address this problem, i.e., the Java platform. Would formal standardization of the Java platform, which was attempted twice but failed, have furthered the aims of portability and scalability? Or could a certain agent technology also have solved the problem? Figure 4 may help identify the different options.

In large technical systems, matching compatibility strategies with flexibility objectives may become a complex matter because the choice of strategy will depend partly on factors such as

• whether the system environment is very dynamic (if not, then a dedicated solution rather than a multi-party standard may suffice);

• for what period the solution is foreseen (i.e., how long the overall system is likely be useful); if necessary for the short term, a dedicated solution can suffice; if longer, a more durable solution such as standardisation and modularity may be better;

• at what system level(s) flexibility can be achieved. Can it be achieved at different levels? Does the type of flexibility differ per level, and should the compatibility solution at these levels therefore also differ?

Conclusion

Compatibility is a core issue in the evolution of large technical systems. Where socio-technical entrenchment appears to hinder a transition, standards and other compatibility strategies are important to look into. They can be a means to (re)create the flexibility required for change.

In this paper, I emphasised that different strategies exist for creating compatibility. These strategies can be plotted as coordinates in a three-dimensional space of compatibility, with the dimensions standardisation, modularity and interactive compatibility.

Matching types of flexibility objectives with compatibility strategies cannot be done in a uniform way. Although some strategies generally seem better set to increase system responsiveness to sustainability demands than others (e.g., highly modularised, modelled consensus standards), the ideal match depends on the circumstances (e.g., what system level is targeted, whether the pressure for change is likely to persist, etc.).

The foregoing illustrates that addressing compatibility problems in an early stage of system design is crucial for the degree of system flexibility later on. In a pre-conditional manner, the chosen compatibility strategy co-determines the ease with which change can take place. Technology innovation policies of governments and companies should therefore take compatibility issues into account, and incorporate a standards—or rather compatibly—policy.

Some very fundamental research questions remain to be answered. Are the three compatibility dimensions proposed the most relevant ones? How generalisable are they and the flexibility objectives to other LTSs?

Tineke M. Egyedi (PhD, 1996) is senior researcher Standardization at the Delft Institute for Research on Standardization. Her current research interests include how standards affect innovation. She has participated in several EU projects (e.g. Study on the specific

policy needs for ICT standardisation) and science foundation projects. She publishes widely. Her most recent book is on 'Inverse Infrastructures' (2012).

She has organised and chaired several conferences, and is regularly invited internationally as a speaker. In 2009 she initiated 'Setting Standards', a simulation exercise currently used by NIST to train US policy makers and earlier by NEN for Chinese standardizers. She is vice-president of the European Academy for Standardization, Fellow of the Open Forum Academy, expert to UN/ECE WP 6, and member of ISICT/ IEEE ComSoc's Emerging Technologies Committee.

Four Dimensions Affecting Policy Resistance In It Procurement

By Mathieu Paapst

The Dutch strategic IT plan "Netherlands Open in Connection" intends to give a direction for public sector buyers to adopt a positive policy and strategy towards open standards, Open Source Software and the use of ODF. This article describes the support and resistance of the policy by government buyers found after researching the documents of 80 tenders, and after interviewing 15 government buyers. In this article the awareness knowledge threshold and four dimensions are described that together can function as an interpretative framework helping policy makers understand why an IT-related policy is supported or resisted. The four dimensions in the proposed framework establish the relative advantage that will influence the degree of willingness to adopt and use a new strategic IT policy. When there is a negative influence within a dimension the policy maker should counterbalance that influence by using a positive instrument within that same dimension.

Introduction

In December 2007 the Dutch government agreed on the action plan Netherlands Open in Connection, hereafter called NOiV, the Dutch acronym. The objectives of this strategic plan are the following:

1. increase interoperability by accelerating the use of open standards;

2. reduction of supplier dependence through a faster introduction of open source software, open standards and the use of ODF (a document format based on an open standard);

3. promotion of a level playing field in the software market (...) by forceful stimulation of the use of open source software, and by giving preference to open source software during the process of IT acquisition.

To reach these goals the action plan describes a number of different policies for open standards and open source software. A vast number of these policies directly affects the process of IT procurement within government organisations. To understand why some objectives are supported and some are resisted by government buyers, the following question for a PhD research was selected: How and under what circumstances does a strategic IT plan influence behaviour regarding the practice of public tenders? If these circumstances can be identified it would become possible for policymakers to take them into account while designing future strategic IT policies. It would also become possible to make predictions about the expected performance of existing strategic IT plans like the European digital agenda[63] or the British Government ICT strategy.[64]

Research And Methodology

To answer the research question a conformance and performance research methodology is used (Maarse, 1991). This

---

[63] http://ec.europa.eu/information_society/digital-agenda/index_en.htm

[64] http://www.cabinetoffice.gov.uk/sites/default/files/resources/uk-government-government-ict-strategy_0.pdf

methodology focuses bottom-up on the influence a strategic policy has on the behaviour of a targeted organisation during the policy implementation phase (Barret, 2004). A strategic policy is fulfilling its purpose if it plays a tangible role in the choices of the addressed policy takers (Faludi, 2000). Through monitoring information is produced about the observed policy outcomes (conformance) and through evaluation the research produces information about the value of the observed policy outcomes (performance).

Monitoring

To see how the Dutch strategic IT policy is enacted in practice, empirical quantitative research was carried out which asked for the data of all the Dutch calls for tender, published in Tenders Electronic Daily (TED) between January and June 2010, that followed the open procedure and that consisted of the delivery of software of some kind.[65] Out of the total sample of 94 calls, data relating to 80 tenders was received, a response rate of 85 %. All these tender documents were examined on different aspects and policies, such as the needs or want for open standards, vendor-independent award criteria, the possibility to use ODF for the bid, and the possible preference for open or closed source products. The goal of this quantitative research is not to generalise the outcome, but to see if during a certain period the policy has been supported or resisted. The collected data from this quantitative research is needed to give input and meaning to the

---

[65] The tenders that asked for Voice over IP technologies or printer hardware with printer drivers were not included in the sample of 95 tenders due to technical expertise limitations.

subsequent question why the strategic policy is resisted or supported (De Lange, 1995).

Evaluation

The quantitative research provides insight into the expected effect of policy decisions in IT procurement. It does not provide insight into the arguments and reasoning behind this application or into the resistance of the policy. It also does not provide an answer to the question whether any found compliance is a direct result of the policy or might be the result of something else. It is not possible to evaluate policy outcomes without establishing that it is an outcome in the first place (Dunn, 2008). To identify these factors further qualitative research was needed within organisations in order to look into the so-called black box of decision-making (Hertogh, 1997). That qualitative research was done during the period between January and April 2011 through in-depth semi-open interviews with 15 respondents in different organisations selected from the quantitative research. These respondents were all public sector buyers with an expertise in IT procurement.

Quantitative Results

The following results emerged from the quantitative research of some Dutch policies:

Policy 1: The use of open standards falling under the CorE principle

The Comply or Explain principle, in short CorE, primarily intends to give a direction for organisations in the (semi-) public sector to adopt and use a certain (open) standard within a specific domain or application area. The selection of these standards and domains is done and published by the Dutch Standardisation Board.[66] In practice it means that within a procurement process the contracting authorities are expected to ask for these specific open standards when applicable (Comply) or otherwise should explain in their annual report why they did not ask for them. This policy helps standardisation within the public sector and supports interoperability.

The quantitative research revealed that the Comply or Explain principle was applicable in 56 cases and a specified open standard should have been asked. Out of these 56 cases there were 20 cases (36%) in which the tender documents followed the policy and actually mentioned a need or want for one or more open standards. In the remaining 36 cases (64%) the CorE standards were not requested. In the annual reports no formal explanation has been published by the noncompliant organisations.

Request for open standards	Frequency	Percent
Yes	20	35.7
No	36	64.3

Table 1: Frequency of needs and wants for CorE open standards

Policy 2: The use of ODF

Open document formats are important for the exchange and processing of documents within organisations. Citizens and businesses should therefore have the possibility to send and receive documents to and from organisations in the (semi-) public

---

[66] www.forumstandaardisatie.nl

sector using the ODF format (ISO 26300). According to the action plan all the ministries and subsidiary government bodies should have been able to receive documents in the ODF open standard by January 2009 at the latest.[67]

In the quantitative research the possibility of a vendor using the ODTODT (ODF) format for his bid was considered. It was found that in almost half (45%) of the cases (n=80) the use of ODF was actually possible. In the other 46 % it was not possible; however this was mainly caused because the contracting authorities demanded the use of the PDF format. Only in one case both PDF and ODF were not possible because a vendor was obliged to use a Microsoft Word and Excel format suitable for Windows XP.

In the 7 remaining cases (9 %) a digital bid was not requested by the tendering organisation.

Possibility of using ODF	Frequency	Percent
Yes	36	45
No	37	46.2
n/a	7	8.8

Table 2: Frequency of possibilities to deliver the bid in ODF

These results suggest at first sight that this particular part of the Dutch policy is in fact supported by the contracting authorities.

Policy 3: Creating a level playing field.

---

[67] Actionplan Netherlands Open in Connection, p.9 http://www.whitehouse.gov/files/documents/ostp/opengov_inbox/nl-in-open-connection.pdf

To guarantee that providers of open source software will get the opportunity to make a competitive offer there ought to be a 'level playing field' for the open source software providers and the closed source software suppliers.

In the quantitative research the tender documents were examined for a preference for closed source software and in particular a preference for a named closed source product or vendor. The mere use of a trademark or product name in public procurement (which is actually a widespread practice [68]) was not, by itself, considered sufficient to demonstrate such a preference. In lots of cases trademarks and product names are used to describe both the current architecture, as well as the software the new solution has to integrate with.[69] For the purpose of this study such a use of trademarks and product names was not believed to establish a clear preference for a product or vendor, although one could argue that it becomes a discriminating preference the moment compatibility is required with previously purchased proprietary software, especially if the technical specifications

---

[68] See e.g. OpenForum Europe, 2011. "OFE Procurement Monitoring Report: EU Member States practice of referring to specific trademarks when procuring for Computer Software packages and Information Systems between the months of February and April 2011", where 147 out of 441 tender notices mention trademarks in procurement documents . http://www.openforumeurope.org/

[69] According to Gosh 2010, this might not be a legitimate functional requirement according to article 23 (8) of the Directive 2004/18/EC since software can usually be described in terms of standards and functionality.

needed for that compatibility are not publicly available and freely usable.[70]

For the purposes of this study actual discriminatory use of trademarks, patents, types, and legal and technical conditions in relation to the vendor or product which was the subject of the procurement needed to be present in order to establish a preference for closed source vendors or products. In 29 cases (36 %) a clear preference for a named closed source product or a closed source vendor was found. Accordingly, other vendors than the preferred one did not have a fair chance to win a bid in these 29 cases.

Preference for closed source vendor or product	Frequency	Percent
Yes	29	36.3
No	51	63.7

Table 3: Preference for closed source vendor or product

In two of these 29 cases the tendering organisations specifically mentioned that they had a preference for a named closed source product and vendor.

Finally some of the other criteria that could prevent vendors, and in particular FLOSS vendors, from making a bid and having a fair chance of winning were considered. In 9 other cases indirect

---

[70]   In decision T-345/03 of 12/03/2008 the Court of first instance of the European Community considers that the Commission infringed the principle of equal treatment between tenderers by failing to make available to all the prospective tenderers from the beginning of the tendering procedure the documentation relating to the technical architecture and source code and that that infringement could thus have affected the award of the contested contract. http://curia.europa.eu/

restrictions were found that made it very difficult or impossible for vendors to offer a FLOSS product.

Restrictions preventing fair competition	Frequency	Percent
Yes	38	47.5
No	42	52.5

Table 4: Frequencies of restrictions for Open source software vendors

This shows that despite the Dutch policy and despite the European procurement rules in almost half of the sampled tenders there still is a preference for closed source vendors or products. This preference inevitably results in vendors of open source products not receiving a fair chance to win the bid. From these results one can also draw the conclusion that this particular part of the Dutch policy is resisted, regardless of the fact that also European procurement rules prescribe a fair chance for vendors.

Qualitative Results

When asked for the drivers and barriers all the respondents mentioned at least one or more of the following four reasons why they resisted or followed (a part of) the policy:
1. Technical reasons
2. Legal reasons
3. Financial/economical reasons
4. Knowledge/experience reasons

Comply or Explain policy

With regards to the Comply or Explain policy the respondents did not feel a negative or positive influence of any kind related to technical, legal or experience reasons. All the respondents seem to be positive about open standards. Some of the respondents did, however, mention that the board of their organisation adopted their own version of the government policy on open standards, which could indicate that there is an additional positive influence. Some of the respondents argued that asking for open standards would most certainly cause vendors to demand a higher price. That idea alone was enough for them to resist the policy. Not all the policy takers resisted or supported the policy deliberately. A rather large proportion of them were simply not aware of the existence of the policy, which could indicate that the government did not communicate enough about the strategic IT plan in general or specifically about the Comply or explain policy. This is also an explanation for the quantitative results that were found.

The use of ODF

Comparing the outcomes of the quantitative research into the possibility to use ODF with the given answers by the respondents gives the following result: The found compliance is not the result of the policy. Only two respondents indicated that they are aware of the existence of the policy. The others said that they have not heard of any policy regarding the use of ODF and that in case no particular format is demanded they expect vendors to use Microsoft formats. When asked about any negative or positive factors the respondents mentioned that their organisations were already *standardised* on the proprietary .doc format. That should, however, not hinder the use of ODF. The government did offer organisations a physical solution in the form of a free USB stick with an ODF converter on it. Within regards to reasons of knowledge and experience some negative influence came from the fact that Microsoft promoted OOXML which made some organisations reluctant in using ODF. As a "countermeasure" the Dutch government supported the ODF-policy with a small communication campaign. In this campaign they called the use of ODF a "right" for citizens in the communication with government organisations, although that right is not based on a specific rule of law, and citizens cannot legally force government organisations to accept their ODF documents. There has not been a negative legal influence. With regards to the financial/economical reasons to follow or resist the policy there are no financial incentives in place. The implementation of the policy however also did not have a significant negative impact on the finances of the organisation.

Creating a level playing field

When asked about the *Creating a level playing field* policy a strong negative influence comes from the fact that organisations are locked in to a technical solution and cannot freely choose to adopt a new technical solution. The respondents feel that the government did not offer a solution in their strategic IT plan to counterbalance this negative influence. Some respondents mention a negative influence with regard to knowledge and experience in the form of misinformation about open source software, most commonly known as fear, uncertainty and doubt (FUD). According to some respondents this is primarily caused by negative experiences in municipalities. Although at first the government tried to do its best to communicate about the positive results of vendor independence through the use of open source software, after some months the focus seemed to shift to other parts of the strategic policy, such as the use of open standards. This may have caused the fact that the positive experiences did not reach the media as much as their negative counterparts. A second negative influence with regard to knowledge and experience is the fact that users within organisations want to work with an IT product they are already familiar with. This subjective compatibility plays a strong role within the decision-making process of most government buyers. Another negative influence felt by the respondents is caused by the so-called switching costs that are considered higher when switching to an open source solution. When it comes to legal reasons some respondents feel a negative influence caused by intellectual property law and running contracts, both protecting monopolists, which makes it in some cases difficult for the respondents to really have a free choice. Despite the fact that according to European procurement law one is not allowed to give preference to a certain vendor, the results from both the quantitative as well as the qualitative research show that the positive influence from this legal driver seems to be heavily outweighed by the negative influence caused by the other reasons.

Interpretative Framework

Based on the research results a theoretical and interpretative framework is constructed that can help policy makers to evaluate (ex post) and forecast (ex ante) IT related policy outcomes.

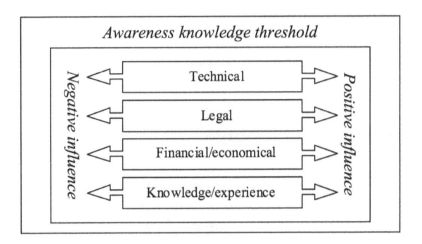

Figure 1: Interpretative framework for strategic IT policies.

Awareness Knowledge

The necessary first step for all strategic policies is that a policy taker needs to be exposed to the policy's existence. In order to be able to support or resist it the policy taker needs to become aware of the policy and the problem the policy is trying to solve. This is called 'awareness knowledge' (Rogers, 2003). The research results clearly show that the awareness knowledge threshold is the most important barrier a policymaker has to address. In at least two cases the observed policy outcomes are not the direct result of the policy performance. This means that the policy maker should think beforehand about possible ways of communicating about the policy to the intended policy taker. Does the policy taker even know that there is a problem and that he or she has to play a certain role in order to solve the problem?

Only after this so-called 'knowledge phase' will the policy taker enter the 'persuasion stage' where a favourable or unfavourable attitude towards the policy will be developed. The policy taker will then try to find out what the advantages and disadvantages of the policy are and in particular what the short-term relative advantage is for his organisation.

The Persuasion Stage

In the persuasion stage the proposed framework describes four dimensions: technical, legal, financial/economical and knowledge/experience. Within each dimensions there can be negative and positive influences that should be taken into account by the policy maker. When there is a strong negative influence within a dimension the policy maker should counterbalance that influence by using a positive instrument within that same dimension. These instruments that the policymaker can use are legal rules, financial compensation/incentives, communication and marketing, and physical solutions (Fenger & Klok, 2008).

Technical dimension:

Within the technical dimension the negative influence is coming from the "objective compatibility" established by current vendors. Vendor lock-in is the situation in which customers are dependent on a single manufacturer or supplier for a product or service and cannot move to another vendor without substantial costs and/or inconvenience. It is that inconvenience that is strongly related to the technical dimension. In the case of IT one must take into account that in most cases there is no greenfield situation. Often an organisation has some sort of legacy where an existing architecture and system are the departure points for future actions. Certain policy choices can be obstructed by technical architecture or technical possibilities (Mifsud Bonnici, 2008). For example new application software must be capable of being installed on the existing platform (e.g. Windows) and must be compatible with the existing applications. These applications usually do not support multi platforms. This headlock also applies the other way around because a new platform must also be able to support the platform-dependent applications already in use. There are also situations in which several applications interweave with each other in a way that makes it impossible to remove an application. With closed source software and closed standards it is difficult to discover how the interaction takes place, but even more difficult to discover how to break free from that 'physical' boundary. A trapped mouse can proclaim that he will stay away from the cheese next time, however that policy will not help him to get out of the mousetrap. To counterbalance the influence of the objective compatibility a strategic IT policy should contain a solution to this barrier. One could think of prescribing certain behaviour by means of technology, or offering an alternative and free product. Both are examples of physical solutions.

Legal dimension:

As soon as a software product (or a standard) has acquired a certain monopoly the supplier of the product is able to exercise additional power on the basis of intellectual property law. The supplier can legally oblige the software user to participate in or to abstain from certain actions. Running contracts could make it impossible to choose a new product or to get the co-operation of the current vendor in creating compatibility with open source software. When the compatibility of products is prevented by exercising the rights of intellectual property or contract law this could also result in an obstruction of competition (van Loon, 2008). This negative legal influence can be counterbalanced by a positive legal influence such as National law, European directives or other forms of legal regulation that can proscribe a certain action. The results from the research do show however that the expected positive influence from this legal driver can be outweighed by the negative influence caused in other dimensions.

Financial/economical dimension:

Not all policy takers will be very supportive of a policy that will cost the organisation money. This specifically applies to government buyers who see it as their primary goal to get good value for money (Arrowsmith & Kunzlik, 2009). Because of the technical dependence on the current software the costs of a migration to a new innovation from a different vendor will in most cases be higher than a migration to a product of the current supplier. Moreover there are possible migration costs resulting from the fact that users need to learn to use a new product. These migration costs can be the reason to resist a policy. This is the financial/economical dependence. This negative influence needs to be counterbalanced by the policy maker using financial incentives, such as government grants.

Knowledge/experience dimension:

In this dimension the perceived subjective compatibility and the communication about the use of the policy can have both a negative and positive influence on the decision to resist or support the policy. The perceived subjective compatibility is the compatibility of the policy or the policy outcomes with the personal experience the policy taker has with a certain technology. The policy taker is also being influenced by the opinions and experiences of his social network. Just like the people in his social network the policy taker wants to work with technology he is already familiar with or with technology that has benefits due to network effects. Any policy that wants to change or challenge that subjective compatibility should address this issue and take the relevant constraints into account.

Policy makers often use communication as a policy instrument (Fenger & Klok, 2008). Within this particular dimension the use of communication can establish the so-called 'how-to knowledge', where a policy taker needs to understand how to use a policy and the 'principles-knowledge', where a policy taker gets an understanding of the principles behind the policy. This policy instrument usually focuses on the use of a policy and results in the production and communication of guidelines or good practices. This particular form of communication will however not establish awareness knowledge. If the policy taker is not aware of the problem and of the policy that tries to solve that problem, he will not be receptive or looking for the *how-to knowledge* or the *principles-knowledge* (Rogers, 2003).

Conclusion

The four described dimensions together establish the relative advantage that will influence the degree of willingness to adopt and use a new strategic IT policy. Together with the awareness knowledge threshold they can function as an interpretative framework helping policy makers understand better why an IT-related policy is supported or resisted. Based on the proposed framework a reasonable hypothesis for further research would be that the desired performance of a strategic IT policy is only possible if the policy maker addresses the awareness knowledge threshold and takes all relevant constraints within the four dimensions into account. The research results show that in the case of the Dutch action plan this has been partially disregarded by the policy maker. The policy maker should think beforehand about possible ways of communicating about the strategic policy to the intended policy taker, and the policy itself should at least contain, announce, or support the use of one or more policy instruments within the four dimensions. When there is an expected negative influence within a dimension the policy maker has to counterbalance that influence by using a positive instrument, preferably within that same dimension. The research results of the *creating a level playing field policy* clearly indicate that for instance the mere use of the legal instrument (e.g. the European procurement guidelines) is not enough to change behaviour and to counterbalance negative influences coming from within the technical dimension and the experience/knowledge dimension. Although it might prove to be possible to use legislative measures or financial investments as a positive instrument within one dimension to counterbalance a negative influence in another dimension, the instrument needs to be strong enough to convince the policy taker that there is a relative advantage big enough to disregard the negative signals coming from the other dimensions.

References

1. Arrowsmith, S. & Kunzlik, P. (2009). Social and environmental policies in EC Procurement Law, Cambridge: University press.

2. Barret, S. (2004). Implementation Studies: Time for a Revival? Personal Reflections on 20 Years of Implementation Studies. In Public Administration 82 No. 2, pp 249-262.

3. Dunn, W.N. (2008). Public policy analysis, New Jersey: Pearson Education.

4. Faludi, A. (2000). The performance of spatial planning. In Planning Practice and Research 15-4, pp 299-318.

5. Fenger, H.J.M. & Klok P.-J. (2008). Beleidsinstrumenten, In Hoogerwerf, A. & Herweijer, M. (Eds.) Overheidsbeleid, Deventer: Kluwer.

6. Gosh, R. (2010).Guidelines on Public Procurement of Open Source Software, Brussels: IDABC.

7. Hertogh, M.L.M. (1997). Consequenties van controle, The Hague: VUGA.

8. De Lange, M. (1995). Besluitvorming rond strategisch beleid, Amsterdam: Thesis Publishers.

9. Van Loon, S. (2008). Licentieweigering als misbruik van machtspositie, Amsterdam: DeLex.

10. Maarse, J.A.M. (1991). Hoe valt de effectiviteit van beleid te verklaren? In Bressers J.th. A. & Hoogerwerf A. (Eds.) Beleidsevaluatie, second edition, Alphen aan den Rijn: Samson HD Tjeenk Willink,122-135.

11. Mifsud Bonnici, J.P. (2008). Self-regulation in cyberspace,

12. The Hague : T.M.C. Asser Press.

13. Rogers E.M. (2003). Diffusion of innovations. London: Simon & Schuster Ltd.

Dr. Mathieu Paapst LLM works as a lecturer and researcher at the department of legal theory, section Law and IT of the University of Groningen. He is interested in the legal, ethical and sociological aspects of the information society. He graduated with a Master's degree on Law and ICT and he received his PhD on a multidisciplinary research project (Law, Public Administration, Innovation and Technology Management) regarding open source and open standards policy resistance in IT procurement. He has been project coordinator and/or researcher for several Dutch research projects (e.g. on standardization policy compliance for the Dutch ministry of Economic Affairs, on semantic interoperability standards for the ministry of Justice, and on e-Case management, an international research for the judicial organizations). He is chief editor of the Ars Aequi Law book on Dutch Internet law, and editor of the academic journal "Tijdschrift voor Internetrecht". He is a board member of the Internet Society (ISOC-nl), and a member of the Dutch governments Commission of procurement experts.

E-Governance in Public Sector ICT Procurement: What is Shaping Practice in Sweden?

By Björn Lundell[71]

Is it reasonable to require any person or organisation to purchase specific software in order to be able to communicate with a governmental organisation? This question is at the heart of an ongoing debate in many countries within the EU, because of its implications for accessibility, transparency, democracy, and fairness in procurement and markets. In this paper we consider the inability of many Swedish governmental organisations to communicate in open formats, and report on an investigation into policy formulation which has led to this situation in one sector – local government. We conducted a survey of all municipalities in Sweden. The final response rate was 99%, after 4 months and a maximum of 7 reminders. We find that there is little or no evidence of consideration given to document formats when procuring software. And in a large majority of cases, there is no documentation of any decision process. Further, organisational adoption of application suites seems more influenced by tradition and a desire to upgrade existing IT

---

[71] Reprinted from Lundell, B. (2011) e-Governance in public sector ICT procurement: what is shaping practice in Sweden?, European Journal of ePractice, 12(6). The text is subject to a Creative Commons Attribution-Noncommercial-NoDerivativeWorks 2.5 licence. The original text can be found at http://www.epractice.eu/en/document/5290101 and the full licence can be consulted at http://creativecommons.org/ licenses/by-nc-nd/2.5/

infrastructure than by any form of analysis and evaluation prior to purchase. In several municipalities specific applications are even named in procurements, which is in conflict with EU directives. There is also considerable confusion amongst respondents related to the difference between application and file format. We make a number of recommendations. Evaluation of document formats should always precede decisions on application and should include interoperability and lock-in considerations. Municipalities must take responsibility for the evaluation of both document formats and office applications before adoption. Further, when assessing the total cost of ownership the analysis should include consideration of exit costs in the procurement. The study highlights a lack of strategic decision making with respect to accessibility, and a resultant lack of transparency with respect to ICT procurement.

Introduction

In a public speech in Brussels, Neelie Kroes, then European Commissioner for Competition Policy, stated that

"No citizen or company should be forced or encouraged to use a particular company's technology to access government information." (Kroes, 2008)

In a strange twist to this statement, a report commissioned by the Swedish government (SOU, 2010) on access to public information states that:

"It is not reasonable to require an authority to purchase new software to be able to provide information in electronic form."

Does this represent a stand-off between the rights of an individual and the rights of government organisations? Or does it represent a natural tension which needs to be resolved technically? A clue is contained in the same report:

> *"Even if an agency discloses a public document in electronic form, it is irrelevant to the individual if that disclosure is made in such a way that he or she cannot access that information in readable form."* (SOU, 2010)

To resolve this tension, then, there is a need to separate out the issue of software purchase – with the reasonable concern about public authorities having to maintain many systems to allow provision of documents in any requested format – from the issue of accessibility of document content. In interoperability terms, this reduces to a need for agreed standard formats, which can be supported by many software products provided on many platforms. This chimes with the recommendation from the Swedish archiving association TAM-Arkiv (TAM, 2010) for long-term access to documents, namely:

> *"<u>Never</u> use vendor dependent formats for long term storage if you can avoid it, because they often are too unstable, too unstructured, and with dependencies to different suppliers' business strategies."* (stress as in the original)

The recommendation stresses the difficulty of assessing how long proprietary formats will be supported and finds them unsuitable for long-term storage. In fact, for decades organisations in the public sector have been concerned about the need for "avoiding vendor lock-in when procuring IT infrastructure." (Guijarro, 2007, p. 91)

With growing recognition of the problems associated with reliance on proprietary formats, there is a commensurate growth in calls for the use of open standard formats for document interchange. An important principle underlying the idea of an open standard is that it ensures that data can be interpreted independently of the tool which generated it. This is one of the main reasons behind the recommendations of the FLOSSPOLS (2005) project that: *"open standards should be mandatory for eGovernment services and preferred for all other procurement of software and software services."* In line with this, we note that policies on using open document formats in the public sector have been adopted in a number of European countries, including two of Sweden's neighbouring countries: Denmark (Denmark, 2010; ITST, 2010) and Norway (Regjeringen, 2009a; Regjeringen, 2009b).

With the adoption of such policies it is clear that there are European countries that expect software companies to adopt open standards "if they want their products to be used by the government." (Fairchild and de Vuyst, 2007, p. 150) One major justification for this is clear: when people want to "interact with government, in either their role as a citizen or a member of a business, they want to do so on their own terms." (Borras, 2004, p. 75)

Over the years, public sector organisations have used a range of different open and proprietary document formats. ODF (ISO/IEC 26300:2006) and PDF/A (ISO 19005-1:2005) are two open standard formats, which have been recognised as international standards (by ISO) and as national standards in many countries. Both formats have been adopted and implemented by different providers of software systems. Two examples of proprietary file formats are IBM's RFT-format and Microsoft's doc-format.

Open standards have been discussed by researchers and policy makers for a long time (e.g. Bird, 1998; EU, 2004; SOU, 2009). An *open standard* (EU, 2004; SOU, 2009) is a *standard* which has certain *open* properties. Such standards can be used as a basis for implementation in software systems under different (proprietary and open source) software licenses. A standard is "a published document that contains a technical specification or other precise criteria designed to be used consistently as a rule, guideline, or definition." (BSI, 2010) When a standard is published and its *technical specification* contains sufficiently detailed information it can be used as a basis for implementation in software applications. For example, the ODF document format has been implemented by several providers using different (proprietary and open source) software licenses (e.g. OpenDoc Society, 2011). On the other hand, the specification of the published Office Open XML standard (ISO/IEC 29500:2008) contains references to external web pages (referring to one specific company's own web site) which are not available. We note that these formats and standards have been extensively discussed (e.g. Brown, 2010; MacCarty and Updegrowe, 2009; Tsilas, 2008), but acknowledge that an analysis of this discussion is beyond the scope of this paper.

From a legal perspective, Swedish and European law for public procurement aims to achieve procurement practices that stimulate a fair and competitive market based on the important principles of transparency, non-discrimination and equal treatment (Directives 2004/17/EC and 2004/18/EC). These directives clarify the public procurement process and how technical specifications can and shall be used in such processes. An important basis is that technical specifications "shall afford equal access for tenderers and not have the effect of creating unjustified obstacles to the opening up of public procurement to competition". Further, a technical specification "shall not refer to a specific make or source, or to a particular process, or to trade marks, patents, types or a specific origin or production with the effect of favouring or eliminating certain undertakings or certain products." (Directive 2004/17/EC (Article 34) and Directive 2004/18/EC (Article 23)). Only on an "exceptional basis" (e.g. when functional requirements cannot be described and for a subject-matter for which there is no international standard) public procurement may refer to specific trade marks and products, but procurement of document formats and office applications is not such an exception.

In this paper, we first consider the recorded situation with respect to support for open document formats in Swedish governmental organisations. We then report on a new study of policies on document formats and ICT procurement related to office document processing. The objective is to understand the influences behind established practice in decision making in Swedish municipalities, and hence help to explain earlier findings of a lack of engagement with the issue of document formats.

Background

An earlier study investigated the level to which Swedish local authorities, health regions and governmental organisations were unable or unwilling to process an ODF file sent to them (Lundell and Lings, 2009). ODF was chosen as an exemplar of an open document format which some European governments insist on being supported by their organisations.

Less than a quarter of local authorities responded to the ODF questionnaire; more than two thirds of respondents acknowledged that they were unable or unwilling to open the document sent to them in ODF. More than a third listed no open formats as preferred for receiving documents. However, a large majority endorsed proprietary formats for such communication.

A part of the investigation was into policies related to the document formats which were accepted. It was found that an understanding of document formats as separate from products using those formats was very low, and there was a surprising and worrying lack of associated policies and strategies available. Only 4 percent claimed to have a policy on accepted document formats, and of these the majority simply endorsed a proprietary format.

Policy making was found not to be transparent, with practice left to the influences of managers and technicians. There is also an evident gap between what public organisations have stated publicly about receiving documents in open formats and what those same organisations do in practice. There were authorities which claimed to accept communications in ODF, but were amongst those failing to open the ODF document sent. The majority which did open the ODF document responded to the questions in a proprietary format.

A second investigation looked at practice in local government with respect to electronic records of important board minutes (Lundell and Lings, 2010). These are not legally required to be archived in electronic form; the only legal requirement is for each municipality to maintain paper copy of the minutes of that board. It was therefore considered to be a good indicator of practice in the absence of a legal requirement.

In the study, minutes were requested, in their electronic form, for the executive boards. It was emphasised that the documents should be supplied in their stored format. The following minutes were requested from each: the most recent board meeting; a meeting from ten years ago; the oldest stored electronically. This gave a perspective on availability and the document formats used. It was found that there are already significant gaps in the electronic archives.

No municipality was found to have a policy with respect to maintaining electronic copy of executive minutes. In the absence of a direct duty to preserve electronic copy, paper copy is still overwhelmingly seen as the only archive medium. This is in spite of the fact that Sweden is considered amongst the most advanced countries in e-Government.

Where electronic copy is kept, it was found that proprietary and closed formats are overwhelmingly used for public documents. This was the case even though there was experience of losing access to documents because of formats which were no longer supported. Further, there was no evidence that the situation was changing. No municipality provided a document in a reusable, open standard document format, in stark contrast with stated central Government vision.

In fact, in its 2004 IT bill (2004/05:175), the Swedish government declared that the use of open standards should be promoted (Regeringen 2005; EU 2005). We also note that the responsible minister for Swedish municipalities has expressed support for open standards as defined in European Interoperability Framework version 1.0 (Odell, 2009), which has also been adopted in the Swedish e-Government strategy (SOU, 2009). Further, based on a legal analysis by the Swedish Association of Local Authorities and Health Regions, there is a recommendation that citizens should be allowed to communicate with members using the established open standard ODF (Lundell and Lings, 2009; SALAR, 2007; SALAR, 2008).

Research Method

The research question addressed through this study is the following. Given that certain document formats are preferred by municipalities in Sweden, to what extent are these preferences informed by policies, either related to document formats or to software procurement?

The question is made easier to answer in Sweden, which has a very strict policy on governmental responses to questions: all questions must be responded to. We sent an email in plain text to each municipality (290 in all), with follow-up reminders sent over a three month period. The email contained six requests.

In the first section, the municipalities were asked about document formats, specifically the format actually used by each municipality in their earlier communication with us. The first was a request to supply any policy or strategy document related to sending out documents in the specified format. The second was a request to inform us of any organisational decision behind the use of the specified format, and to supply any documentation. The third asked for information about any planned revisions to working practice.

The second section related to software procurement, and in particular that related to software for writing office documents. The first two requests were for factual information about the application primarily recommended within the municipality: what is it and when was it (or an earlier version of it) first introduced into the organisation? The third was a request for the documented decision (along with any other related documents) for the most recent procurement related to the application.

The study resulted in both quantitative and qualitative data. Quantitative data was analysed to gauge the overall position with respect to informed decision making about document formats and office applications. The text of responses, together with that of any supplied documents, was analysed qualitatively, to give some insight into the real state of practice.

Responsiveness To The Questionnaire

The request email was sent to the registered address of each municipality. A municipality is required to respond promptly (at least with an acknowledgement), usually interpreted to mean within 24 hours. If no response was received within a working week, then a reminder was sent. This continued with, after the second reminder, increased emphasis that the email included a request for public documents that they are required by law to respond to.

This resulted in the response profile shown in Figure 1.

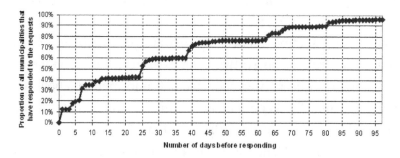

Figure 1: Evolution of response rate over time

As can be seen, 20% (59) of the municipalities responded to the initial request within 3 working days. A reminder elicited further responses, resulting in a 42% response rate (122) after 3 weeks. After a second reminder, the majority (59%) had responded. The final response rate after 4 months was 99%. Overall, a maximum of 7 reminders was used, although many further interactions were required to probe more deeply when initial responses were inadequate. Four municipalities failed to respond.

Some delays were evidently caused by confusion over who should respond, no individual feeling able to respond to all requests. This meant that the email was circulated within the organisation. In some cases this resulted in partial answers being given from different parts of an organisation – primarily a split between answers to the two sections of requests. The second section was often answered by the ICT department. This even resulted in different responses being made to the same request by different people within the same organisation. In a small number, one ICT department served several municipalities. This caused initial confusion over whether an individual response had been made on behalf of more than one municipality.

A few municipalities explicitly declined to respond and some provided partial responses, which were probed further. It is possible that some people interpreted the email as a survey and missed the fact that it contained explicit requests for public documents. A few spent time on a response refuting their obligation to respond. In these cases, a simpler request for the required documents was sent (with reminders) which did elicit some responses.

We estimate that, for a well organised authority, it should take less than ten minutes to respond to the email (we have anecdotal information which reinforces this), so it is unlikely that resource demand was a significant factor in a decision not to respond, or in an extreme delay in responding.

Observations From The Analysis

Few municipalities have a documented policy regarding the use of document formats (see Table 1).

Documented policy for document format exists?	Percentage of municipalities
Responded yes	2%
Responded no	95%
Decline to respond	3%

Table 1: Existence of a documented policy on document formats

Only 2% of all (290) Swedish municipalities claimed to have a documented policy for the practice of sending out documents in the specific formats used by their municipality. By far the majority (95%) specifically responded that there was a lack of documented policy/strategy. The remaining 3% declined to respond.

In total, 19% of all municipalities supplied documents in response to our request for evaluations and decisions related to document formats and office applications. However, only 8% of all municipalities supplied relevant documents. Among the documents considered not to be relevant were web publication policies; layout instructions; and instructions for how to write documents. It should be noted that no municipality provided a TCO analysis which considered exit costs related to a possible selection of a proprietary document format.

A clear majority (92%) of all municipalities recommend and support MS Office as the primary office application in their municipality for writing office documents; 5% of all municipalities did not mention any office application, or declined to respond on this point.

Most municipalities primarily recommend and support only one office suite for writing office documents. Overall, 86% of all municipalities only recommend and support MS Office in their administration, and 3% only recommend and support OpenOffice.org. A number of municipalities recommend a combination for their own administration: 5% a combination of MS Office and OpenOffice.org, and 1% a combination of MS Office and StarOffice. Another 4% recommend MS Office for their administration, but OpenOffice.org for (some or all of) their schools (see Table 2).

Preferred office suite (tools) for writing office documents	*Percentage of preference by respondents*
MS Office	86%
OpenOffice.org	3%
MS Office & OpenOffice.org	5%
MS Office & StarOffice	1%
MS Office (for administration) & OpenOffice (for schools)	4%

Table 2: Preferences for office applications

With few exceptions, municipalities do not undertake any evaluation of either document formats or office applications before adoption. For example, one municipality responded:

> "No formal, political decision exists; neither is there any documentation or evaluation."

Further, the lack of a documented decision related to the selection or procurement of an office application is common to most municipalities. In some, decisions are taken locally with roll-out throughout the organisation without any evaluation: "The decision was taken by our IT advisory board; no direct evaluation was done. An organisation-wide adoption was made for all units."

In some municipalities, the lack of documented evaluations and decisions make the authority defensive, so that except for supplying a copy of the signed contract with their supplier they refuse to elaborate: "Referring to the above, we report that the *procurement of our office suite was done through the Select Agreement. We decided on Microsoft Office and attach the agreement with Microsoft. We decline to answer your queštions."*

Of the municipalities claiming to do some kind of evaluation, most seem totally dependent on processes for IT procurement provided by central agencies for public sector procurement in Sweden, such as Kommentus and Kammarkollegiet. For example, such dependency is clearly illustrated in this response from one municipality: *"There has been no local procurement as we participate in SKL Kommentus AB's and Microsoft's Select Agreement."*

These central agencies are dedicated to supporting municipalities and other public sector organisations by establishing central contracts from which each municipality calls off licences for office applications. For example, one municipality cites the evaluation performed by the central agency in their response on evaluation, stating that they *"have used the coordinated procurement of software (Microsoft Select) by Kommentus since the mid-1990s. Common evaluation criteria include price, delivery times and other parameters."* From their complete response it was made clear that the evaluation performed by Kommentus has been their only evaluation, which implies that they have been dependent upon this centrally performed evaluation for around fifteen years. Several municipalities gave similar responses. There is evidence of a common view that some form of evaluation of the office application itself (i.e. the product) is being performed in such central procurement activities.

However, the evaluation of office applications undertaken by Kammarkollegiet and Kommentus does *not* address functionality, licensing or pricing of office applications. Instead, their evaluation is entirely focused on evaluating the reseller. Hence, even if a municipality signs such a central procurement agreement, there is still a need for them to undertake their own evaluation and analysis of document formats and office applications in order to assess the product before adoption.

Amongst the municipalities that actually have undertaken evaluations that consider file formats, one responded that a decision was made *"to standardise on file format, rather than product."* A few municipalities report that they have initiated work on developing a policy for document formats: *"We are working on developing a policy document that describes how and in what format external document are communicated. We will certainly decide that documents that should not be edited must be in PDF format and others must be sent in a non-proprietary format, RTF or possibly ODF. Today we have .doc as the document default."*

Overall, we found that a clear minority (1%) of all municipalities have considered format prior to purchasing office application.

Amongst municipalities that have evaluated applications there are mixed views on applications, and outcomes of evaluations differ. For example, a municipality that evaluated OpenOffice.org found that it fulfilled their needs: *"Since OpenOffice has all the required features and also implied a financial saving the choice has not been difficult."* On the other hand, a municipality that introduced MS Office concluded differently and recommended MS Office 2007 after their evaluation: *"[Microsoft Office] was introduced in the mid-1990s and was evaluated in 2007, along with OpenOffice 2.4 ... Primarily we recommend MS Office 2007."* This further reinforces the need for local evaluation.

From the responses it was clear that there is considerable confusion amongst respondents related to the difference between application and file format. Amongst the responses concerning application, respondents mentioned specific names of suppliers and applications (in almost all such cases the responses included one or both of "Microsoft" and "Word"), whereas in other cases responses referred to specific versions of a specific office suite (e.g. "MS Office Word 2007"). Regarding responses for file formats, respondents mentioned suppliers (e.g. "Microsoft"), applications (e.g. "Word"), and formats (e.g. "Microsoft formats"), and in several cases initially gave incomplete, unclear, and confused responses. In general, from the number of requests for clarification (via email and over the telephone) we note that many respondents do not see a difference between applications and a file formats.

Most municipalities primarily focus their attention on adopting an office application; the file format issue is treated as a consequence of the application choice. For example, one municipality responded that they consider applications as standards and have decided to use these with their 'default' file formats: "*[The municipality] views Microsoft Word and Adobe (i.e. doc and pdf) as de facto standards and has chosen to use them without major evaluation.*" Several others acknowledge that they lack a policy on document formats, but respond that the choice of format is implicitly determined from the choice of application: "*We do not have any specific document that regulates document formats. Instead it is determined over time by monitoring the software version agreed within the municipal organization.*" Yet other municipalities report that, without a decision, they just use the 'default' format which is supported by their application: "*there is no written decision with regard to document formats, but in practice .docx is the default setting.*"

A number of municipalities have a practice of renewing licenses. Renewal of licences is usually being done without evaluation, perhaps over many years. In many cases, the procurement decision dates from a very long time ago. In other cases, municipalities use centrally procured agreements for renewal of licenses (so it is not considered a new procurement). For example, one municipality responded: "*We have not bought the software, rather we have held licenses since 1992. These licenses have been extended since then and upgraded on a continuous basis. No procurement was done in 1992.*" A different municipality adopted a proprietary product and the office suite has not been evaluated since then: "*In 1997 it was decided that the municipality would use the zac-concept (zero management concept) which is a Microsoft-oriented approach. Since then, the Microsoft platform has not been evaluated. Procurements that we do therefore are for MS Office licenses.*"

Evaluation of file formats and office applications for a municipality cannot be undertaken in isolation of already adopted IT-systems due to various kinds of potential lock-in problems. Therefore, any evaluation and adoption of an office suite needs to consider other systems which have already been adopted. Several responses in the survey indicate that other systems already in use in the municipalities are perceived to dictate requirements on the document format and the office application. Hence, the responses indicate several examples of different kinds of lock-in scenarios, including format lock-in and vendor lock-in. Most such systems require the proprietary .doc format, which makes migration to the open document format (ODF) difficult. For example, one municipality responded that "*many of the IT systems that we already use, or that we intend to procure within the administrative sections, are integrated with, and in some cases totally dependent on, functionality and components in MS Office.*"

Interoperability is critical for municipalities, but several responses indicate that such vendor lock-in is problematic. As illustrated by one respondent: "*Today, suppliers of enterprise support systems to the municipalities are tightly tied to Microsoft software. This means that in practice it is very difficult to use open source software to break the hegemony that exiSts."*

In many municipalities a different policy is adopted in schools since interoperability problems related to other legacy systems in the municipality is less of an issue. Overall, our responses indicate that in municipalities where there is less perceived lock-in they are more open to alternatives, as illustrated by this response from one municipality: *"Within adminiStration, where application providers have selected the Microsoft track, we are forced to use their office suite. In schools, only OpenOffice is used."* Other responses showed that evaluation for schools in some cases is based on other factors for office applications: *"the discussion at the time was that Microsoft had the largeSt market share amongSt companies and municipalities and that it was a good platform for Students to learn"*

The practice of sending out and receiving documents varies. Although several municipalities accept PDF there is a clear dominance of using proprietary document formats. For example, one municipality responded that: *"We send out documents in the format in which it is easieSt to send them. In moSt cases, this is .pdf or .doc."* Two municipalities go so far as to expose, on their public website, which formats they accept: *"[XXX] municipality can only receive files which are in one of the following formats: .doc, .txt, .pdf, .xls"*

There is evidence of a limited but increasing awareness of issues related to document format and application options, including archiving. Some municipalities are beginning to separate out the issue of application from format, and are looking towards archiving needs, as illustrated by this response: *"Open, platform independent, and archive secure file and document formats are important."*

In addition to the vast majority of municipalities that use the proprietary .doc format for external and internal communication there is also a small group using ODF as a format for internal communication. One municipality responded: *"If you are intending to send internally, it must be in ODF format."* However, in this group .doc is still used for communication with citizens. Amongst municipalities that have adopted ODF, responses show an awareness of the need to be flexible and behave accordingly, as illustrated by the response from one municipality: *"Internally, we use ODF. In external contact with partners, we are flexible and can adapt to who we are corresponding with, such as using .doc, etc."*

Recommendation For Practice

According to the results of the study, municipalities (or some other national public sector organisation) must take responsibility for the evaluation of both document formats and office applications before adoption. Evaluations should be conducted according to the specific needs of each municipality and its outcome should always be documented. A municipality cannot and should not solely rely on central purchasing organisations for setting policy and for analysis of their own requirements.

Any decision based on evaluation outcomes should be documented, and renewal of licenses should be treated in the same way as an initial procurement. Further, evaluation should be undertaken on a regular basis, and at least before each major adoption decision. Education policy should not be dictated by such things as current market share for office applications.

Evaluation of document formats should always precede decisions on application and should include interoperability and lock-in considerations. Enterprise support applications should not be procured if they dictate the use of a specific proprietary document format or office application. Further, when assessing total cost of ownership the analysis should include consideration of exit costs in the procurement.

Long-term digital archiving is a significant issue for both municipalities and citizens. It is tightly coupled with formats, both for preservation and long-term accessibility. A decision on formats is a policy decision, and must not simply be considered as a 'technical' issue that follows from an adoption of a specific office application. Municipalities should standardise (and base their procurements) on open formats, not on specific office applications.

Citizens should not be expected to buy proprietary software in order to communicate with municipalities; any policy on format must specifically address this point, and also any implications of differences between external and internal communication practices. From this, we recommend that citizens must be able to communicate with municipalities using open formats.

Conclusions

This paper has reported on problems for many Swedish governmental organisations to communicate in open formats. It specifically reports from an investigation into current practice and policy formulation which has led to this situation in one sector – local government.

There are many reasons for the reported problems, including a lack of leadership, awareness and know-how amongst practitioners and those responsible at different levels in Swedish municipalities and other public sector organisations.

Most municipalities do not undertake (or even initiate) an evaluation before procurement of software and adoption of document formats. In responses, reference is often made to central procurement agencies, and a number of municipalities seem to misinterpret both the scope and focus of evaluation undertaken by those agencies.

Further, it seems that purchasing of application suites is largely a matter of history rather than strategic decisions. In some municipalities specific applications are named in procurements, which is in conflict with EU directives. This implies that many municipalities have made themselves over-reliant upon central agencies.

Each policy/strategy document received from a municipality was analysed to reveal how policies and strategies related to document formats were considered. However, some municipalities provided documents which did not cover document formats, and some responses indicated considerable confusion.

In conclusion, we find that there is little or no evidence of consideration given to document formats when municipalities procure software. In a large majority of cases there is no formal evaluation underpinning procurement decisions and no documentation of decisions. The study highlights a lack of strategic decision making with respect to accessibility, and a resultant lack of transparency with respect to ICT procurement.

References

1. Bird, G. B. (1998). The Business Benefit of Standards, StandardView, 6 (2), 76-80.

2. Borras, J. (2004). International Technical Standards for e-Government. The Electronic Journal of e-Government, 2 (2), 75-80.

3. Brown, A. (2010). Microsoft Fails the Standards Test, March 31, 2010, http://www.adjb.net/post/Microsoft-Fails-the-Standards-Test.aspx.

4. Denmark (2010). Konklusionspapir om anvendelsen af åbne standarder for software i det offentlige. Ministry of Science Technology and Innovation, January 29, 2010, http://vtu.dk/filer/aabne-standarder/bilag58.html *(in Danish)*.

5. EU (2004). European Interoperability Framework for pan-European eGovernment Services, European Commission, Version 1.0, retrieved (22 January 2008) from http://ec.europa.eu/idabc/servlets/Doca2cd.pdf?id=19528.

6. EU (2005). From an IT policy for society to a policy for the information society, Näringsdepartementet, published by the Regeringskansliet, June 30, 2005, http://books.google.se/books?id=7BEzMQAACAAJ.

7. Fairchild, A. & de Vuyst, B. (2007). Governmental Collaboration and Infrastructural Standards in Belgium. The Electronic Journal of e-Government, 5 (2), 145-152.

8. FLOSSPOLS (2005). An Economic Basis for Open Standards, Deliverable D4, December 12, 2005, http://flosspols.org.

9. Guijarro, L. (2007). Interoperability frameworks and enterprise architectures in e-government initiatives in Europe and the United States. Government Information Quarterly, 24 (1), 89-101.

10. ITST (2010). Common understanding on the use of open standards for software in the public sector. National IT and Telecom Agency, Ministry of Science Technology and Innovation, January 29, 2010, http://www.digst.dk/Arkitektur-og-standarder/Standardisering/AAbne-standarder-politisk-baggrund/Konklusionspapir/Common-understanding-on-the-use-of-open-standards-for-software-in-the-public-sector.

11. Kroes, N. (2008). Being Open About Standards. Brussels, June 10, SPEECH/08/317, European Commissioner for Competition Policy.

12. Lundell, B. & Lings, B. (2009). Openness to Standard Document Formats in Swedish Public Sector Organisations. In Boldyreff, C. (Ed.) Open Source Ecosystems: Diverse Communities Interacting, IFIP Information Federation for Information Processing, Vol. 299, Berlin: Springer, 320-329.

13. Lundell, B. & Lings, B. (2010). How open are local government documents in Sweden? A case for open standards. In Agerfalk, P. et al. (Eds.) Open Source Software: New Horizons, Berlin: Springer, 177-187.

14. MacCarthy, M. & Updegrove, A. (2009). Competition in Office Suite Programs, Unpublished Manuscript, May 11, retrieved (12 January 2011) from: http://www18.georgetown.edu/data/people/maccartm/publication-43095.pdf.

15. Odell, M. (2009). Innovations for Europe: Increasing Public Value, European Public Sector Award, Public Speech, Maastricht 5 November, 2009, http://www.regeringen.se/sb/d/ 11678/a/134858.

16. OpenDoc Society (2011). OpenDoc Society, retrieved (12 January 2011) from http://www.opendocsociety.org/.

17. Regeringen (2005). Regeringens proposition 2004/05:175 – Från IT-politik för samhället till politik för IT-samhället, Prop. 2004/05:175, Stockholm, June 30, 2005, http:// www.regeringen.se/sb/d/108/a/47411 (in Swedish).

18. Regjeringen (2009a). Nye obligatoriske IT-standarder for staten vedtatt, Fornyings- og Administrasjonsdepartementet. Press release: July 2, 2009, http://www.regjeringen.no/nb/dep/ fad/pressesenter/pressemeldinger/2009/nye-obligatoriske-it-standarder-for-stat.html?id=570650 (in Norwegian).

19. Regjeringen (2009b). Referansekatalog for IT-standarder i offentlig sektor, Ministry of Government Administration, Reform and Church Affairs, Version 2.0, June 25, retrieved (22 December 2009) from http://www.regjeringen.no/nb/ dokumentarkiv/stoltenberg-ii/fad_2006-2009/nyheter-og-pressemeldinger/pressemeldinger/2009/nye-obligatoriske-it-standarder-for-stat.html?id=570650 (in Norwegian).

20. SALAR (2007). Digital sopsortering: Att hantera skräppost i kommuner och landsting, Swedish Association of Local Authorities and Health Regions, December, ISBN: 978-91-7164-296-7 (in Swedish).

21. SALAR (2008). Lagrummet: Hantering av bifogade filer, Swedish Association of Local Authorities and Health Regions, 11 January, retrieved (8 February 2009) from http:// www.skl.se/artikel.asp?A=50260& C=6621 *(in Swedish),* website now defunct.

22. SOU (2009). Strategi för myndigheternas arbete med e-förvaltning, Statens Offentliga Utredningar: SOU 2009:86, e-Delegationen, Finansdepartementet, Regeringskansliet, Stockholm, retrieved (19 October 2009) from http:// www.sweden.gov.se/content/1/c6/13/38/13/1dc00905.pdf *(in Swedish).*

23. SOU (2010). Allmänna handlingar i elektronisk form - offentlighet och integritet. Statens Offentliga Utredningar, SOU 2010:4, Regeringskansliet, Stockholm, retrieved (13 April 2010) from http://www.sweden.gov.se/content/1/ c6/13/90/17/0de3bc8e.pdf *(in Swedish).*

24. TAM (2010). Rekommendation - Format för långtidslagring. Version 1.0, March 11, Bromma:TAM-Arkiv, retrieved (16 April 2010) from http://www.tam-arkiv.se/pdf/ TAM5-2010_FormatLangtidslagring_1_0.pdf

25. Tsilas, N.L. (2007). Enabling open innovation and interoperability: recommendations for policy-makers. In Janowski, T. and Pardo, T.A. (Eds.) Proceedings of the 1st international conference on Theory and practice of electronic governance (ICEGOV '07), New York: ACM, 53-56.

Dr. Björn Lundell has been researching the Open Source phenomenon for a number of years. He co-lead a work package in the EU FP6 CALIBRE project (2004-2006) and was the technical manager in the industrial (ITEA) research project COSI (2005-2008), involving analysis of the adoption of Open Source practices within companies. He is the project leader for the Open Source Action (OSA)-project (2008-2010), and the project leader for a Nordic (NordForsk) OSS Researchers Network (2009-2012). His research is reported in over 60 publications in a variety of international journals and conferences. He is a founding member of the IFIP Working Group 2.13 on Open Source Software, and the founding chair of Open Source Sweden, an industry association established by Swedish Open Source companies. He was the organiser of the Fifth International Conference of Open Source Systems (OSS 2009), which was held in Skövde, Sweden.

FOSS Governance And Collaboration: From A Good Idea To Coherent Market Approach

By Shane Coughlan[72]

Free and Open Source Software (sometimes called Open Source or FLOSS, and referred to in this paper by the commonly used term FOSS) is an approach to software that emphasises the freedoms provided to end users. Originally formulated in 1983 by a computer scientist concerned with access to technology, it has become a central component of mainstream IT. The popularity of FOSS has produced a wealth of related terminology and perspectives which occasionally lead to confusion about what it actually is and what are the best ways to engage with the field. This paper will address such confusion by providing a clear overview of FOSS, how it works, and why it is successful. It will go back to first principles in defining FOSS, explaining the concept of licensing that underpins it, and examining how this paradigm facilitates multiple development and business models. The key assertion is that the productive application of FOSS relies on good governance and active collaboration. While it is difficult to determine which precise governance model (or models) may be best suited to the long-term sustenance of FOSS as an approach to developing knowledge products, the indicators provided by the previous two decades

---

[72] Reprinted from Coughlan, S. (2011) Journal of Economics, No. 29 (Special Issue), The Facility of Law and Literature, Shimane University, Japan.

suggest that FOSS governance will continue to be effectively refined by its stakeholders.

Defining And Understanding FOSS

Free and Open Source Software (FOSS) is an approach to software that facilitates multiple development and business models. It is best characterised as a software paradigm. A software paradigm (also referred to as a software model) helps contextualise how stakeholders will create, distribute and/or use the software on computers. There are different software paradigms that compete for attention, investment and market-share in the modern business environment. The two predominant software paradigms are termed proprietary and FOSS, with the criteria for differentiation being based on the level of control over software that each facilitates. With proprietary software, control tends to lie primarily with the vendor, while with FOSS control tends to be weighted towards the end user.

The Origin Of FOSS

FOSS originated in the USA during the early 1980s. While in the early years of computer science it was common for people to share software relatively freely, the concept of selling software untied to physical hardware had begun to change this practice. What is termed the 'Software Industry' started in the early 1960s, and by the late 1970s it had grown significantly, due in no small part to the development of the personal computer in the mid-1970s and the rise of companies such as Microsoft.[73] The

---

[73] http://en.wikipedia.org/wiki/Software_industry

tension between those who wanted to share software technology and those who wanted to charge for access to software is illustrated by a letter Bill Gates wrote to the Homebrew Computer Club in 1976.[74] Entitled 'An Open Letter to Hobbyists', it charged that the practice of sharing code damaged the ability of people to produce good software.[75]

In 1983 Richard Stallman, an employee at MIT's Artificial Intelligence laboratory, decided to formalise the concepts behind the sharing of software technology. He founded a project to create a complete FOSS operating system that was compatible with Unix called the GNU Project.[76] This project also necessitated the development of terminology to describe how and why the FOSS paradigm worked.[77] In 1985 this emerging 'Free Software Movement' consolidated with Mr Stallman's establishment of the Free Software Foundation, the formal publisher and maintainer of the first and the most popular FOSS licences.[78]

The Definition Of FOSS

FOSS is not simply an aspiration to share software. It is a formally defined set of attributes applied to compliant software. The full definition of FOSS is hosted on the GNU Project website.[79] A concise overview is provided by Richard Stallman in his 2002 book, 'Free Software, Free Society':

---

[74] http://en.wikipedia.org/wiki/Open_Letter_to_Hobbyists

[75] Ibid.

[76] http://www.gnu.org/

[77] http://en.wikipedia.org/wiki/Free_software

[78] http://www.fsf.org/

[79] http://www.gnu.org/philosophy/free-sw.html

"The term "Free Software" is sometimes misunderstood—it has nothing to do with price. It is about freedom. Here, therefore, is the definition of Free Software: a program is Free Software, for you, a particular user, if:

• You have the freedom to run the program, for any purpose.

• You have the freedom to modify the program to suit your needs. (To make this freedom effective in practice, you must have access to the source code, since making changes in a program without having the source code is exceedingly difficult.)

• You have the freedom to redistribute copies, either gratis or for a fee.

• You have the freedom to distribute modified versions of the program, so that the community can benefit from your improvements." [80]

These four freedoms have been simplified in certain ways to illustrated the benefits of the approach. On the front page of the GNU Project website it suggests that "To understand the concept, you should think of "free" as in "free speech", not as in "free beer"."[81] Another is to shorten the four freedoms themselves into the form of 'use, study, share and improve.'[82]

---

[80] http://www.gnu.org/philosophy/fsfs/rms-essays.pdf (page 26)

[81] http://www.gnu.org/

[82] http://lwn.net/Articles/308594/

Challenges To Foss From Incumbent Market Interests

In 2000, Steve Ballmer, Chief Executive Office of Microsoft, famously likened FOSS to Communism.[83] Its advocates would counter that the FOSS movement is not and has never been a movement against the principles of financial gain nor is it inherently anti-corporate. Rather the opposite, in the sense that FOSS explicitly and purposefully allows commercial exploitation.[84]

This being said, Richard Stallman contends that key stakeholders in early software production were acting a way that he found unethical. He felt they were abusing their position and by doing so abusing the users of computers. But this assertion is less of an anti-market stance than an observation regarding inefficiency and control (given, of course, that we assume markets are intended to serve the majority participating rather than a narrow group who control supply and demand):

> "The modern computers of the era, such as the VAX or the 68020, had their own operating systems, but none of them were Free Software: you had to sign a non-disclosure agreement even to get an executable copy.
>
> This meant that the first step in using a computer was to promise not to help your neighbour. A cooperating community was forbidden. The rule made by the owners of proprietary software was, "If you share with your

---

[83] http://www.theregister.co.uk/2000/07/31/ ms_ballmer_linux_is_communism/

[84] http://www.fsf.org/licensing/essays/selling.html

neighbour, you are a pirate. If you want any changes, beg us to make them."

The idea that the proprietary-software social system—the system that says you are not allowed to share or change software —is antisocial, that it is unethical, that it is simply wrong, may come as a surprise to some readers. But what else could we say about a system based on dividing the public and keeping users helpless? Readers who find the idea surprising may have taken this proprietary-software social system as given, or judged it on the terms suggested by proprietary software businesses. Software publishers have worked long and hard to convince people that there is only one way to look at the issue." [85]

Stallman's issue could be described as what people now may term 'lock-in' and 'market distortion.' His perspective has since been validated in two critical ways, one being the recent spate of anti-trust cases and the other being the wholesale commercial adoption of FOSS precisely because it facilitates competition, market growth and the maximisation of investment.

Those involved in FOSS did not historically perceive it to be an extreme movement but rather to be a different to software from what an incumbent group of self-interested parties wished. Professor Laurence Lessig sums it up well with his introduction to 'FOSS, Free Society':

"there are those who call Stallman's message too extreme. But extreme it is not. Indeed, in an obvious sense, Stallman's work is a simple translation of the freedoms that our tradition crafted in the world before code. "Free Software" would assure that the world governed by code is

---

[85] http://www.gnu.org/philosophy/fsfs/rms-essays.pdf, page 24.

as "free" as our tradition that built the world before code."
86

It is reasonable to suggest that some parties who were extremely worried about FOSS invested a lot of money and time trying to challenge its rise in the technology market. One reason for this is that FOSS as a paradigm presents a significant challenge to proprietary software as a paradigm. Proprietary software depends on charging per-copy licence fees to derive the majority of its profit while FOSS imposes no per-copy licence fees. The difference between the models can be worth millions of dollars in upfront fees.

Those working to challenge FOSS's credibility during its ascendancy to a market-leading position ultimately failed for a simple reason. FOSS is an approach to software that allows people to do a great deal with code. Some people - usually computer scientists like Richard Stallman - understood that FOSS was a good idea in its early days. Some people - perhaps those from portfolio management or sales backgrounds - took longer to understand the benefit. Nowadays all types of parties in all types of segments tend to see and derive some value from FOSS.

Underﬆanding FOSS Means Underﬆanding FOSS Licenses

The concept of FOSS describes a way to use, study, share and improve software, though this alone does not equate to providing the formal structure required for its potential to be realised. Stakeholders need to derive and maintain value regardless of their status of collaborators or competitors, and this leads us inevitably

---

to the common rules - rather than general concept - by which FOSS transactions are managed. These rules provide a framework that underpins the realisation of expectations in the field.

The goals of FOSS are realised through licences governed by copyright law. These licences take a different form compared to traditional proprietary documents. Instead of providing a narrow grant of use with a long list of exceptions and restrictions, they tend to provide a broad grant of use with few restrictions. But each license differers slightly in the grants it provides, and a common challenge for adopters of FOSS relates to what licence is beneficial for their situation.

FOSS licences are often divided into three categories by its advocates and users; non-Copyleft, weak-Copyleft and strong-Copyleft. Therefore Copyleft - while not inherent to Free Software - is perhaps the most important distinguishing features to categorise FOSS, and is one of the best places to start when one seeks to understand how such licenses work.

As with the definition of Free Software, Copyleft was first defined by Richard Stallman. He wanted to ensure that the GNU Operating System would be available to people with the four freedoms he had identified as being important, and he wanted to ensure this availability would continue in the mid-to-long-term.

> "The goal of GNU was to give users freedom, not just to be popular. So we needed to use distribution terms that would prevent GNU software from being turned into proprietary software. The method we use is called copyleft.
>
> Copyleft uses copyright law, but flips it over to serve the opposite of its usual purpose: instead of a means of privatising software, it becomes a means of keeping software free." [87]

---

[87] http://www.gnu.org/philosophy/fsfs/rms-essays.pdf, page 28.

Copyleft says that the freedoms provided with the software apply to all subsequent users of the software as well. Copyleft is not an inherent characteristic of FOSS, but rather a way of maintaining a set of grants applied to the software in question. This is a distinction sometimes overlooked by people new to FOSS, leading to confusion when encountering FOSS licences that provide the ability to use, study, share and improve code according to the formal definition of the Free Software Foundation, yet not containing Copyleft provisions.

Some would suggest that non-Copyleft licences are best because the cooperative model does not require formal statements of subsequent sharing.[88] Some maintain that they want an explicit Copyleft requirement applied to their code.[89] Some parties like the Free Software Foundation advocate the use of strong-Copyleft whenever possible.[90] Perhaps the most useful guide for adopters with a pragmatic perspective is popularity. The form of licence is used by over 50% of FOSS are strong-Copyleft licences such as the GNU GPL.[91] It is most notably used on the Linux kernel,[92] most of the GNU Project,[93] and other critical technologies like SAMBA.[94] This is probably because strong-Copyleft provides a very predictable and stable grant for the technology, allowing

---

[88] http://www.onlamp.com/pub/a/onlamp/2005/06/30/esr_interview.html

[89] http://www.freesoftwaremagazine.com/columns/why_i_choose_copyleft_for_my_projects

[90] http://www.fsf.org/licensing/licenses/why-not-lgpl.html

[91] http://www.BlackDucksoftware.com/oss

[92] http://en.wikipedia.org/wiki/Linux

[93] http://en.wikipedia.org/wiki/GNU

[94] http://us6.samba.org/samba/docs/GPL.html

multiple parties to cooperate in using and developing it over prolonged periods.

Understanding The Most Popular Foss License

The GNU GPL is a very popular FOSS licence, accounting for over half of the total FOSS licence use according to BlackDuck Software research.[95] The most widely used variant of the GPL is version 2 of the licence, though version 3 – released in 2007 – is becoming increasingly popular and has been adopted by major code projects like SAMBA.[96] It was created to encapsulate the four freedoms applied to FOSS as effectively as possible for current and future users, and for this reason it is also a strong-Copyleft FOSS licence. Its purpose has never been otherwise, as Stallman's description of its origin attests:

> "The specific implementation of copyleft that we use for most GNU software is the GNU General Public License, or GNU GPL for short." [97]

Some parties have taken issue with the way that the GPL contains a preamble that explains its originals and purpose, and that this makes it a political manifesto as well as a legal document.[98] But one could equally argue the preamble is measured and makes clear what the document is, as evidenced by - for instance – its first paragraph in version two of the licence:

---

95   http://www.BlackDucksoftware.com/oss

96   http://news.samba.org/announcements/samba_gplv3/

97   http://www.gnu.org/philosophy/fsfs/rms-essays.pdf, page 29.

98   http://www.netc.org/openoptions/background/history.html

"The licenses for most software are designed to take away your freedom to share and change it. By contrast, the GNU General Public License is intended to guarantee your freedom to share and change FOSS--to make sure the software is free for all its users. This General Public License applies to most of the Free Software Foundation's software and to any other program whose authors commit to using it. (Some other Free Software Foundation software is covered by the GNU Lesser General Public License instead.) You can apply it to your programs, too."[99]

While there is little doubt that organisations such as the Free Software Foundation have a political agenda, FOSS licences such as the GPL are no more impacted by this then the licences of proprietary companies are impacted by those parties having a financial interest in the market. The aims of issuing entities and the inherent validity of the licenses they issue are two different matters.

As FOSS grew into a mainstream approach in IT, questions were raised about whether the primary licence used, the GNU GPL, was actually valid.[100] These questions suggested that the model applied by FOSS was not something that worked in copyright law, and were immediately contested by essays produced by figures central to FOSS development.[101] Later they were contested more substantially through court cases against parties infringing the GPL licence in Europe.[102] These cases resulted in court victories, and were followed by events in the

---

[99] http://www.gnu.org/licenses/gpl-2.0.html

[100] See for example Andrés Guadamuz (2004) '*Viral Contracts or Unenforceable Documents? Contractual Validity of Copyleft Licenses*', E.I.P.R. Vol. 26, Issue 8, pp.331-339. Also online at http://papers.ssrn.com/sol3/papers.cfm?abstract_id=569101

[101] http://www.gnu.org/philosophy/enforcing-gpl.html

[102] http://gpl-violations.org/news/20040519-iptables-sitecom.html

USA that further validated the licensing approach[103] and its effectiveness in being applied to commercial transactions.[104]

Today there is little doubt the GPL is a valid legal document. Version 2 is well-entrenched in the market, and the growing use of version 3 has occurred despite some criticism of the document while it was being drafted.[105] This may be indicative that such criticism, as with criticism directed at earlier versions of the GPL or at FOSS itself, was largely unfounded. It is also possible to suggest that criticism of the GPL provoked responses, elaboration and clarification that contributed to maturing the licence, and perhaps the paradigm as a whole.

The Governance Of FOSS

The Internet has allowed people to communicate and to work together across great distances at a lower cost and at a higher speed than ever before. It has been a powerful driver in reducing barriers to working with partners and customers to accomplish goals, what is sometimes referred to as co-innovation.[106] In the software field it is difficult for a single vendor to meet all the requirements of multiple customers, and it is more effective for several parties to cooperate on developing and enhancing a shared platform. This is what increasingly happens, and it has lead to the commercial sustainability of FOSS projects such as the Linux

---

[103] http://www.fsf.org/news/wallace-vs-fsf

[104] http://www.softwarefreedom.org/news/2007/oct/30/busybox-monsoon-settlement/

[105] http://www.eweek.com/c/a/Linux-and-Open-Source/Latest-Draft-of-GPL-3-Comes-Under-Fire/

[106] http://theotherthomasotter.wordpress.com/2007/05/03/co-innovation-is-a-strength-not-a-weakness/

kernel.[107] This is because FOSS, a software paradigm built on the inherent assumption of cooperation and sharing, is a natural beneficiary of the global trend towards increased cooperation.

One good example is the Linux kernel, which started as a student project,[108] and has grown into the core of an operating system used in a wide variety of fields with financial backing from companies like Fujitsu, Hitachi, HP, IBM, Intel, NEC, Novell, and Oracle.[109] Linux is GPL software designed to run on many types of computer, and it is developed through a world-wide cooperative project on the Internet.[110] Given its scale and success, it provides an excellent example of co-innovative development inside the FOSS paradigm. It is structured into teams with leaders who consolidate work, and a handful of key developers that then combine the components into the final product. There is a relatively low barrier to entry regarding participation in development, and each individual stakeholder will have their own reasons for investing in the project. What is noticeable is that the collective output of the parties collaborating is stable, reliable and widely used in critical industries.

Cooperation As A Lasting Mechanism For Change

Cooperation in creating software has profound implications for development models and the management of processes, and

---

[107] http://linuxfoundation.org/en/Members

[108] http://www.linux.org/people/linus_post.html

[109] http://linuxfoundation.org/en/
FAQ#Who_are_members_of_the_Linux_Foundation.3F

[110] http://www.kernel.org/

has expanded far beyond the concept of working with a small, select group of similar companies. That was a template of interaction tied to the Industrial Revolution, and appears archaic in a world where instant communication allows an individual in Shenyang, China to work as effectively as one in London. Modern cooperation requires the broad sharing of information and tools without delay between multiple parties and even legal entities, with an emphasis on reducing access time further to optimise the benefit of cooperation. An increasing number of formal models have been emerging to facilitate this, with one example being 'Agile software development,' which places emphasis on the feedback provided by creative participants to guide further development.[111]

Such cooperative development is arguably permanent for two reasons, one systemic and one market-based. From the systemic perspective, the reduction of barriers and costs to cooperation have lead to a self-sustaining cycle where new development models have emerged that increase the efficiency of cooperation, and in turn foster further optimisation and investment in such activity. From a market perspective, users are requiring more complex and interconnected software, and without unlimited engineering resources, the most efficient way to produce such software is through building shared platforms with other market participants.

The dynamics of the software industry have altered in the last two decades. Twenty years ago the dominant proprietary paradigm resulted in a small number of providers controlling innovation and serving a large number of users in a fairly static relationship. However, the emerging FOSS paradigm encouraged new development models and new software development processes that moved the decision-making emphasis to users.

---

[111] http://en.wikipedia.org/wiki/Agile_software_development

Since the FOSS paradigm gained mainstream traction this has had a profound effect on the market as a whole. Increased user involvement in consultation, design, testing and improvement is noticeable in every approach to software today. One consequence of this has been to blur the distinction between what constitutes a user and what constitutes a provider. FOSS notably empowers all users to become providers at any time of their choosing.

The Many Development And Business Models Of FOSS

The proprietary software and FOSS paradigms facilitate the establishment and improvement of various software development models and processes. These development models may be hierarchical, loosely managed or unstructured depending on the given software paradigm and the requirements of the individuals or organisations working on a project. It would be incorrect to associate FOSS exclusively with one development or business model, though new observers or entrants to the FOSS market occasionally do so. This is perhaps a result of limiting their research to a narrow range of case-studies or usage models.

Such misconceptions are partly attributable to an essay by Eric Raymond circulated in 1997 entitled "The Cathedral and the Bazaar,"[112] and extended into a book published by O'Reilly Media in 1999.[113] The proposition that "given enough eyeballs, all bugs are shallow" appeared to suggest that the limited, hierarchical and restricted world of proprietary commercial software ultimately could not compete with the broad, dynamic and more bazaar-like

---

[112] http://www.catb.org/~esr/writings/cathedral-bazaar/

[113] http://oreilly.com/catalog/9780596001315/

world of FOSS. However, it should be understood that Mr. Raymond's paper was not originally a comparison of the FOSS development methodology versus a proprietary development methodology. It was a criticism of hierarchical structures applied by the GNU Project (a FOSS project) versus the more flat management structure of the Linux Project (a FOSS project).[114]

Misunderstandings regarding the organisation and management of FOSS are not isolated to development models. From the perspective of the traditional proprietary software world it can be difficult to understand the approach taken with FOSS, and some parties have questioned its validity as a commercial approach.[115] However, concern with regards viable business models and FOSS tend to arise when parties have a preconception that per-unit licence costs are an inherent requirement to qualify as commercial software. While FOSS allows a wealth of business models to be applied, per-unit licensing costs is not one of them.

Per-unit revenue models would either have to prevent sharing of code to maximise their market and thus undermine one of the four freedoms defined by the Free Software Foundation, or they would be circumvented by users who would have a choice of paying the originator for a copy of the software or getting one from a third-party without cost.

There are many business models applicable to FOSS for the same reason that FOSS facilitates multiple development models; this paradigm provides a broad range of parameters that participants operate inside. Examples of FOSS business models include:

---

[114] http://www.alamut.com/subj/economics/misc/cathedral.html

[115] http://business.timesonline.co.uk/tol/business/industry_sectors/technology/article733264.ece

- Development-related services to produce specialised products, such as bespoke product customisation for enterprises.
- Integration-related services to ensure that products work with existing systems, such as in Enterprise intranets, SME office networks and banking communication systems.
- Support-related services to maintain deployed solutions, particularly in the SME, governmental and enterprises sphere.
- Software as a Service to deliver application functionality over a network, such as in Web 2.0 companies or search companies like Google.
- Cloud computing to deliver processing functionality over a network, such as those provided by companies like Sun Microsystems.
- Mixed-models combining FOSS and proprietary software, such as the product offerings from Oracle with GNU/Linux and their proprietary enterprise database running on top.
- Dual-licensing models where code is released under both a FOSS and a proprietary licence.

The most common FOSS business models in the server and workstation market segment tend to be support provision across multiple products (i.e. like IBM)[116] or support provision for a branded family of products (i.e. like Red Hat).[117] While dual-licensing used to be relatively common, the best known companies such as MySQL and Trolltech did not scale beyond being multi-million dollar enterprises and were instead acquired by multi-billion dollar corporations. Since then the visible side of

---

[116] http://www-03.ibm.com/linux/

[117] http://www.redhat.com/

their business has tended to be focused on the FOSS element of the product offering rather than the proprietary.

Embedded companies (those that make telephones, routers and other small computing devices) now frequently make use of FOSS. The business models applied tend towards mixed-model, with a FOSS platform being used to provide basic services, and perhaps a proprietary series of components to provide a differentiator. The LiMo Foundation's work in the mobile sphere[118] or MontaVista's products in the embedded networking sphere provide examples of this.[119]

In network services there are a great variety of companies using FOSS. Most notable is perhaps Google, which uses FOSS-based technologies to power its infrastructure, and makes a modified FOSS operating system available for its employees workstations.[120] Because Google primarily provides network services, rather than focusing on the distribution of software, the use of FOSS has very little impact on their business model except to reduce costs, and their modifications to FOSS code do not generally have to be distributed. This has come under some criticism as effectively using FOSS without fully participating in the paradigm.[121] However, regardless of what one thinks of their use of the code, Google's business model has proven highly successful. In essence, they used FOSS to facilitate infrastructure that would have cost billions to build as proprietary software for a far smaller sum, and they leveraged this advantage to provide services above the traditional limits of their corporate scale and funding.

---

[118] http://www.limofoundation.org/

[119] http://www.mvista.com/

[120] http://en.wikipedia.org/wiki/Google_platform

[121] http://ostatic.com/blog/google-touts-open-source-cred

Ultimately the number of possible business models applicable to FOSS make it impossible to pick out any one as a clear favourite. As with any field of business, the correct model depends on market segment analysis, an understanding of skills, and a prudent balance between maximisation of profit and sustainability. There is no 'FOSS business model' in the singular sense; the licences used in the field provide broad grants that foster a wide range of approaches.

Understanding The Governance Of FOSS

The early governance of FOSS was understandably centred on the licenses that govern FOSS transactions. There was a narrow focus on compliance because it was regarded as the critical issue for minimising risk in adoption and deployment, and that was the critical issue facing early users. However, as the stakeholders in the field became more sophisticated, so too did their approach to governance, and this lead to a shift in perspective towards understanding governance as a tool to maximise value while honouring obligations. This is a related but wider concept than reducing risk.

For early adopters of FOSS the most common problems encountered can be summarised as having their roots in two key issues; people didn't read the licenses properly, or they read them but didn't follow the terms. The solution to these problems were equally simple; people had to read the licenses in question and follow their terms. Nevertheless, new adopters frequently encountered issues, with some notable cases being GPL-violations.org versus Sitecom,[122] GPL-violations.org versus D-Link[123] and SFLC versus 14 companies.[124] A lack of understanding or a lack of process maturity can generally be proposed as a reasonable explanation for these occurrences.

As FOSS stakeholders became more understanding of how FOSS provides value - namely through collaboration between an ever-changing pool of third parties - they also became more nuanced in their understanding of the governance necessary to provide maximum benefit. This resulted in a shift from policy in the form of lists of accepted or rejected licenses, code or deployment approaches towards more nuanced processes that provided the flexibility to adopt new technology and adapt to changes in licensing or market demands.   This tended to be intertwined with the evolution of participants in how they approach the field as a whole. If one understands the value of FOSS to be found in the collaborative energy centred around common frameworks, then stakeholder maturity will see an increasing shift from relative isolation as an entity to collaboration as a participant in a community.

While early FOSS governance used to be focused on understanding licenses as obligations, the mature governance of FOSS is about the questions that lifecycle management raises, namely "what type of code do you use and why?", "how do you manage change to ensure continual improvement?", "how do you ensure your obligations are met?" and "how is this applied through the supply chain from inception to end-of-life for each product or solution involved?" Stakeholders become more active

---

[122] http://gpl-violations.org/news/20040415-iptables.html

[123] http://www.jbb.de/judgment_dc_frankfurt_gpl.pdf

[124] http://www.linux-magazine.com/Online/News/SFLC-Files-Lawsuit-Against-14-Companies-for-GPL-Violations

buying or developing the processes to manage code, training people internally to obtain value while minimising risk, and doing the same for the supply chain on which they depend. This is a natural consequence of seeking to maximise potential through shared rules to improve collaboration.

The Emergence Of Market Solutions

There are many services, products and collaborative platforms that contribute to governance in the FOSS marketplace. None solves every challenge that the paradigm can raise, but many deliver utility to new entrants and experienced stakeholders alike, providing avenues for minimising risk, improving efficiency and dealing with suppliers or customers. One example is FOSSBazaar, a community for sharing governance data that was initiated by HP via the Linux Foundation, and which continues to over a broad range of general material and commentary today.[125] Others include comprehensive commercial solutions that have appeared from companies like BlackDuck Software[126] and OpenLogic[127] that deliver lifecycle management, the non-profit Linux Foundation compliance programme,[128] and independent FOSS projects like the Binary Analysis Tool.[129]

Collaboration is key to deriving value from FOSS and sustaining it through the development, deployment and support of products or solutions. This is not about code; the collaboration

---

[125] http://www.fossbazaar.org/

[126] http://www.blackducksoftware.com/

[127] http://www.openlogic.com/index2.php

[128] http://www.linuxfoundation.org/programs/legal/compliance

[129] http://www.binaryanalysis.org/en/home

that provides value is not limited to software, but is instead applicable to the approach required to obtain value in the modern market. It translates into platform management, and requires managers, programmers and legal experts to collaborate across organisational boundaries and nation borders.

Interaction and cooperation around stakeholders is far more than an aspiration or ad hoc arrangement in the increasingly mature FOSS-related economy. One example is that the Linux Foundation helps stakeholders collaborate around Linux in the US, Europe and Asia by organising meetings, working groups and conferences to encourage shared understanding and knowledge sharing.[130] Another is the European Legal Network, an invitation-based effort facilitated by Free Software Foundation Europe that helps 280 stakeholders collaborate across 4 continents, and which runs private mailing lists, special interest groups and conferences to share knowledge.[131]

It is impractical to attempt to list the degree to which collaboration - or crowd-sourcing - has permeated the global FOSS economy, but a cursory examination of the Asia-Pacific region is illustrative of how initiatives like the Linux Foundation and the European Legal Network are far from isolated. In Japan collaborative activities are organised by the government via the IPA[132] and the industry via Linux Foundation Japan,[133] while regional organisations like Ruby City Matsue[134] have also fostered

---

[130] http://www.linuxfoundation.org/

[131] http://fsfe.org/projects/ftf/network.en.html

[132] http://www.ipa.go.jp/software/open/ossc/index.html

[133] http://www.linuxfoundation.jp/

[134] http://www1.city.matsue.shimane.jp/sangyoushinkou/open/rubycitymatsue/ruby_city_projecting.html

enough momentum to host international conferences.[135]   In Taiwan, the Open Source Software Foundry gives support and legal advice to help companies use FOSS,[136] and a new legal network modelled on the European Legal Network is also being prepared for launch.[137] In Korea, NIPA is collaborating with KOSS Law Center and FSFE to develop governance activities,[138] with tangible outcomes including the creation of a national legal network and the launch of a new international conference to share knowledge.[139]

Increased Governance And Collaboration Is Driven By The Market

Software is a knowledge product and FOSS is a management approach for this product. FOSS requires effective governance and collaboration to create maximum value for every stakeholder regardless of their individual product range or market segment. The required degree of cooperation is appearing in national, regional and global markets with a growing amount of shared structure visible due to the interconnected nature of the industry. The outstanding question is probably whether this trend will continue or some form of market pressure - be it litigation or alternative methods of deriving value from software proving more

---

[135] http://www.rubyworld-conf.org/en/

[136] http://www.openfoundry.org/

[137] http://osln.tw/doku.php?id=open_source_legal_network_taiwan

[138] http://www.oss.kr/7065

[139] http://www.kosslaw.or.kr/conference/conference01.php

attractive - will lead to a lack of long-term coherent governance for the field.

This is more than an idle question. Research by Gartner previously suggested that 85% of enterprises are already using FOSS in one capacity or another, and the remaining 15% expect to use it within twelve months of the survey.[140] These figures the type of market penetration figures previously suggested by UNU Merit, when in their 2007 report for the European Commission they suggested that "FLOSS-related services could reach a 32% share of all IT services by 2010, and the FLOSS-related share of the economy could reach 4% of European GDP by 2010."[141] Research shows no indication that the growth of FOSS will slow at any point in the near future, given fair market access.

This last point may prove to be crucially important. If competition drives innovation and provides an impartial method of determining the success or failure of product or business models, then it is important for fair and equitable competition to be fostered in markets regardless of the particular approach chosen by participants. It follows that access to information regarding interoperability and interaction between software components is therefore a key requirement in the modern IT market to foster such competition. Conversely, if fair access is not provided, then competitive paradigms like FOSS may be hindered in terms of future market penetration and opportunities despite their potential utility.

FOSS And Standardisation

---

[140] http://www.gartner.com/it/page.jsp?id=801412

[141] http://flossimpact.eu/

FOSS and standardisation is an area that has drawn increased interest in recent years, not least due to the challenges FOSS faces with regards market access and the ability to compete fairly (for a given value of fairly) against older and more established approaches to organising the creation, distribution and support of software knowledge products. This is best exemplified by the public debate over what became known as MS-OOXML, a next generation document format. It was suggested that the process was biased[142] and that the grants provided for the proposed standard were insufficient for FOSS.[143]

A great deal of the discussion surrounding standardisation and FOSS centred on patents. The reason for this are the are fundamentally different goals for patents and standards, as illustrated by Mr Karsten Meinhold, chairman of the ETSI IPR Special Committee, when he stated that "IPRs and Standards serve different purposes: IPRs are destined for private exclusive use, standards are intended for public, collective use."[144] FOSS, being also designed for public, collective use, tends not to fall into the normal categorisation of how IPR is positioned.

Patents in standards had previously been managed by grants such as RAND, and these were considered sufficient for proprietary software. However, that did not mean that such conditions facilitated fair market access and competition for all software paradigms competing in the market. For example, per-unit royalty payments would compromise the freedom of people to share the code, as would terms that did not permit sub-licensing.

---

[142] http://www.linuxjournal.com/node/1000294

[143] http://arstechnica.com/software/news/2008/03/sflc-ooxml-could-poses-patent-threat-to-gpl-licensed-software.ars

[144] http://ec.europa.eu/enterprise/ict/policy/standards/ws08ipr/presentations/21meinhold_en.pdf

Indeed, several FOSS licences have provisions regarding issues like patents to ensure that the four freedoms defined by the copyright licence continue in full to all subsequent users. The GPL is an example of such a licence, and others with the same or similar provisions actually make up the majority of the FOSS paradigm. For example, according to BlackDuck Software research 66.57% of projects use GPL family licences that explicitly prohibit the application of patent restrictions on covered software.[145] Excluding these licences from a standard would mean excluding 2/3 of the FOSS model participants from accessing that standard. That is quite a challenge for FOSS and for markets that seek to be open, competitive and genuinely innovative, though debate still continues regarding the best way to address the matter.

Globalisation And FOSS

Globalisation refers to the process of national economies becoming more open, economics becoming more 'global' than 'national', and to the reduction of national controls over economic matters.[146] In effect, changing the world from a loose organisation of states into a single giant canvas, and providing new opportunities for people to work together. This concept has profound implications for cooperative models of innovation and production, though it is not without its detractors.

The proposition of emerging Globalisation is contested by 'globalisation scepticism', a view summed up by Hirst and Thompson's comment that "the closer we looked the shallower and more unfounded became the claims of the more radical

---

[145] http://www.BlackDucksoftware.com/oss

[146] Ramesh Mishra, *Globalisation and the Welfare State,* (Cheltenham: Edward Elgar, 1999), 3-4.

advocates of economic globalisation."[147] For these sceptics there are international economies but there is no evidence for a truly 'global' economy.[148] This is a valid criticism within the constraints of their definition, but it can equally be contested as relevant only in the context of purely economic, rather than cultural or communicative Globalisation.

Whether one defines Globalisation as an example of increasing global capitalism or as a deeper and more complex mix of political, cultural and financial connections, it suggests that the world is not merely a collection of states with limited communication and sharing potential. From that perspective, and therefore from the perspective of technology and business, it does not matter whether globalisation is a trend towards a global economy or a collection of increasingly interlinked international economies. Knowledge, goods and people are far more mobile now than ever before. Software, a technology that can be easily transferred through communication networks, is one of the greatest beneficiaries of this development. It follows that the current success of FOSS may therefore be partly explicable as a product of such Globalisation, and that it will inevitably continue to expand as long as the trend towards increased human interaction continues.

In this context it is worth noting that the concepts behind FOSS have blazed a trail in developing the norms required for massively distributed collaboration, and they have proven to be influential beyond the field of technology. A key example is that when Professor Laurence Lessig established the Creative Commons, and in doing so formalised an approach to foster

---

[147] Paul Hirst and Grahame Thompson, *Globalization in Question: The International Economy and the Possibilities*, 2nd ed. (Cambridge: Polity Press, 1999), p2.

[148] Ibid, p16.

increased engagement and exchange around cultural artefacts, he drew heavily on the concepts behind FOSS licenses. In the introduction to Lessig's primary book on cultural sharing, 'Free Culture,' he acknowledges that his insights do not exist in isolation, and states:

> "The inspiration for the title and for much of the argument of this book comes from the work of Richard Stallman and the Free Software Foundation. Indeed, as I reread Stallman's own work, especially the essays in Free Software, Free Society, I realise that all of the theoretical insights I develop here are insights Stallman described decades ago."[149]

Conclusion

FOSS is an approach to software that emphasises the freedoms provided to end users, with a particular focus on the ability of participants to use, study, share and improve technology. While occasionally misunderstood as being non-commercial, FOSS has always been conceptualised as something that allows commercial activity. It is framed by its licences, which range from providing a simple, non-perpetual grant of the receiving user freedom (as with the Modified BSD licence) through to providing such freedom in perpetuity via Copyleft and addressing issues such as patents (as with the GPL). While still relatively new, most concerns related to this approach to licensing have been substantially addressed in courts of law, in industry usage and in common understanding over the licence terms and their intent. Today FOSS has become a central component of mainstream IT.

---

[149] http://www.free-culture.cc/freecontent/, page 14.

The popularity of FOSS has produced a wealth of related terminology and perspectives, and this occasionally leads to some degree of confusion or misunderstanding. To address this it is necessary to go back to first principles in defining FOSS, understanding the concept of licensing that underpins it, and examining how it facilitates multiple development and business models. This leads to a number of useful observations. The first is that FOSS is a paradigm that facilitates a multitude of development and business models, barring only those inherently tied to the concept of per-unit software licence fees. The second is that FOSS benefits from globalisation, especially in the context of increasing long-distance cooperation facilitated by the Internet. This applies equally whether one is concerned with cooperation between like-minded professionals or with blurring the distinction between a developer and a user of technology. The third is that the licences that appear to best support this diversity of choice are those that provide both common rules for interaction (i.e. terms of using, studying, sharing and improving) while also delivering a mechanism for sustaining these rules for subsequent users (i.e. strong-Copyleft licences such as the GNU GPL).

Once FOSS is understood as a method of deriving value from knowledge products with an emphasis on collaboration, it naturally follows that its productive application depends on good governance and active collaboration. This type of management structure has been gradually developed by stakeholders using the same methods applied to the creation of creation of FOSS knowledge products. though it is worth noting that the current mechanisms does not fully explain how FOSS potential can be continually realised by an increasingly diverse eco-system of stakeholders. While it is evident that FOSS governance is increasingly sophisticated, it is equally evident that understanding which model is best suited to the long-term management of software is far from trivial in a world with complex supply chains, products deployed across a multitude of legal jurisdictions, and a vast array of stakeholders with a multitude of development, deployment and business models.

However, despite such difficulty in determining which precise governance model (or models) may be best suited to the long-term sustenance of FOSS, the indicators provided by the previous two decades suggest that its management will continue to be effectively refined by stakeholders. FOSS is well positioned because it facilitates sharing and cooperation in a world where such activities tend to easier, cheaper and more effective than ever before. It is therefore reasonable to assert that FOSS will continue to benefit from and drive increased openness and interoperability in the technology market for pragmatic reasons.

In conclusion, as the concepts underlying FOSS are applied to other creative works such as text, music or images, mainstream acceptance of this approach to developing and maintaining knowledge products will increase. Its governance - and therefore sustainability - will be refined as it scales, and any issues will gradually be worked out due to stakeholder requirements and market dynamics.

Shane Coughlan is an expert in communication methods and business development. He is well known for building bridges between commercial and non-commercial stakeholders in the technology sector. His professional accomplishments include establishing a legal department for the primary NGO promoting Free Software in Europe, building a professional network of over 270 legal counsel and technical experts across 4 continents, and aligning corporate and community interests to launch both the first law journal and first legal book dedicated to Free/Open Source Software. He has been part of the OIN licensing team since November 2009 and has lead the team since August 2013.

Shane has extensive knowledge of Internet technologies, management best practice, community building and Free/Open Source Software. His experience includes engagement with the server, desktop, embedded and mobile telecommunication industries. He does business in Europe, Asia and the Americas, and maintains a broad network of contacts.

The Open Versus Closed Debate

By Andrew A Adams

Introduction

When developing information systems, whether they be standalone business process support programs for single machines or internet-spanning user-generated content distribution mechanisms, various choices that need to be made in the specification, design and implementation of that system can be characterised as a choice about openness or closure. Sometimes these choices are binary in nature (open or closed, with no in-between), whereas at others it's the level of open-ness that's the question, with a setting available somewhere between fully open and fully closed. In this paper I discuss the implications of various types of choice for various business scenarios, and their relation to general principles of information ethics, such as those espoused by the Association for Computing Machinery (ACM) and the British Computer Society (BCS) in their relevant codes of ethics.

I begin with a discussion of the business issues to be considered in free software versus proprietary licenses and the question of software idea patents, then consider the issue of communication protocols. The related concept of openness in data formats is presented next, followed by the concept of community rather than customers. A brief case study of the issue of openness in anti-malware information finishes the main body of the paper, with the final section deriving conclusions about the benefits or not of openness in these various fields.

Code

When the words "open" and "closed" are mentioned to software developers, the first ideas to come to mind are almost certainly the license under which a piece of software will be released: a free/open source license or a proprietary one. In addition to the other open or closed elements discussed below, this question itself is not so simple and clear-cut a question as it might appear. In addition to the question of release license, and even this has more to it than a simple consideration, there are also the questions of development environment and the individual rights of members of the development teams, the highly vexing question of software idea patents, and of source code escrow. These questions also need consideration by customers when commissioning software as well as by development organisations.

Software Licenses

Software licensing is a complicated concept. As is well-documented in, for example, Williams (2002), in the early days of computing, software was principally developed by the hardware manufacturers as part of a package of selling expensive hardware to clients, developed for in-house use or developed as part of research by academics. That all changed in the 70s along with the development of personal computers. The growing commoditisation of hardware computing capacity, as always happens with commoditisation, drove down the price of the commoditised good, but also opened up new opportunities for profit in related goods and services. In computing, this new market was principally in programs to run on the machines. By the time Bill Gates was complaining about unauthorised copying

(Gates, 1976) the lines began to be drawn between the proprietary and free software approaches. By 1984, Richard Stallman, already long involved in development of freely shared software such as the Emacs text editor (whose non-legalistic "license" was a social contract and "distributed on a basis of communal sharing, which means that all improvements must be given back to [Stallman] to be incorporated and distributed" (Williams, 2002)) announced the start of a new project: GNU (GNU's not Unix), dedicated to building a free (as in speech) version of the Unix operating system. After much discussion and some soul-searching to find the "sweet spot" for embodying the personal freedom "hacker" (Williams, 2002; Levy, 2001) ideology, the first version of the GNU Public License was produced, setting one of the guiding points of software licensing ever since.

The Scope Of A Software License

Since 1976 in the US[150] computer software has been deemed an artistic or literary endeavour attracting copyright in the individual expression (but not the "actual processes or methods embodied in the program", see below on Software Idea Patents) that embodies that program. It was quickly decided that this extended not only to the source code, which is the actual material written by the programmer, but also to the resulting executable object code. Software is, of course, rather different to other types of written work in that it is useless on its own without hardware on which to run. However, a decent analogy can be made with

---

[150] Following fairly quickly in much of the developed world and more slowly elsewhere.

music which for most people[151] written music is useless without instruments (and for those not musically trained, musicians to play them) on which to execute the sheet music.

Arguments about the legal reach of software licenses have been in progress since the first licenses were issued. When one pays for software, what exactly is one buying? The settled legal view is that software is licensed, not sold. When one "buys" software, one is entering into an agreement whose terms are principally set by the license offered by the owner(s) of the copyright. This license may include restrictions on how many times the software may be installed onto different machines, how many copies may be running at any one time, and certain elements of the usage of the software. However, there are also terms which may not be placed on the purchaser. Users have the right to "decompile" the program for the purpose of "interoperability", that is to figure out how to make other programs communicate with the purchased program. Users generally have the right to sell on a piece of software (in the US, under the "first sale" doctrine (Steffik, 1997) and in the EU under the "exhaustion of rights" doctrine (May, 2003)).

Network Associates Inc. included terms for its Virus Scan software (later in this paper we will discuss anti-malware software as a case study in openness dilemmas) which restricted users' discussion of the capabilities of the program, and in particular its relative benchmark tests. The New York State Attorney General's Office challenged this license as a matter of public policy and won the court case[152] arguing that restrictions such as this were an

---

[151] Terry Pratchett's character Lord Vetinari, who reads sheet music for pleasure without the messy business of musicians getting in the way, aside.

[152] Spitzer v. Network Associates, Inc. dba McAfee Software 758 N.Y.S.2d 466 (Supreme Court N.Y. 2003).

unconstitutional restriction on freedom of speech, not justified in the protection of trade secrets or goodwill. It was further argued that in particular the ability to discuss the capabilities and vulnerabilities (including comparative benchmarking) of security software was an essential public good that could not be over-ridden by contract terms.

As discussed in Chandler (2008), the enforceability of "shrinkwrap",[153] "click-wrap"[154] and "browse-wrap"[155] licenses have come under significant scrutiny, as have attempts to restrict who can use software.

Within the non-proprietary software community there are a range of positions on how to license software. Some claim that any restriction on the freedom of others to do what they will with software is wrong. This idea is embedded in the Berkeley Software Development (BSD) license which simply requires that anyone distributing the source and/or object code acknowledge the original authors' copyright and disclaims any liability. Other, such as the Free Software Foundation (FSF), which develops and maintains the GNU General Public License (GPL) regard the share-alike principle (taking someone else's work, and adding a small amount to it should not allow you to deny similar rights to

---

[153] Software sold in a cellophane-wrapped box, the details of the license being inside the box and stating or implying that opening the cellophane wrapping constitutes agreement to the license.

[154] A software license whose terms are presented to the user when they attempt to install the software. Typically, the user must select an "I agree" box or similar in order for the installation to proceed.

[155] A software license approach legally discredited in the US by Specht v. Netscape No. 01-7860 (L) (2d Cir., October 1, 2002). A license appears somewhere on a web page which also includes a link to download the software thus licensed.

your users) as paramount to maintaining a free information infrastructure. Contrary to the belief of some, the GPL does not constrain programmers to distribute their amendments, nor does it prohibit charging for providing the amended code. In practice, however, anyone who does charge could easily find their business model undermined by a single paying customer who chooses to then pass the software along without charging a fee. The GPL does require that the amender gives the redistribution and derived work production rights to anyone to whom they distribute the software. There are those who argue that the GPL is not a "free" enough license, as mentioned above, and that by imposing the share-alike principle they are infringing on others' rights. There are others who argue that the GPL is not restrictive enough, but still in the name of "freedom". Thus there are licenses such as the "Hacktivismo Enhanced-Source Software License Agreement" which attempts to prohibit governments (in particular) from distributing amended versions of their software which have been altered to allow government spying on citizens' computer usage. (see www.hacktivismo.com/about/hessla.php).

The Ethics And Business Of Choosing A License

The example of Microsoft (MS), which started complaining about unauthorised copying[156] of their software in 1976 and today are one of the world's largest companies, would seem to dictate that the only sensible business decision to make when writing software is to use as strong a proprietary license as one can, and even to reach as far into restricting competition as to limit the free speech of users with respect to discussing any possible failings of the software with others. However, as presented below, even for commercial operations and sound financial reasons, a strong proprietary license may not be the best choice even for commercial software producers. For individuals and organisations commissioning software, or having software written in-house and/ or by contractors the issue is even more blurred.

In some ways it is unfortunate that the unpaid community effort element of the Hacker Ethic (Raymond, 2001; Loren, 2004) has come to represent free software as a concept so strongly. The volunteer hacker working on software in their free time, donating their time and expertise for the altruistic good of the community,

---

[156] Piracy is a hideous crime involving the armed hijack of a vessel at sea and the theft of the cargo and even the vessel itself often while employing savage violence against the crew and any passengers. The link between this heinous crime and unauthorised copying of material under copyright is one drawn by those who cannot justify the status of their holding of copyright, and who must label the act of copying as something so hideous that no one can argue against it as the only way of winning their case. The author is with Richard Stallman on this usage and therefore describes it technically as unauthorised copying. Even the "illegality" of such an action is uncertain in many cases without deep examination of the circumstances — not all unauthorised copying is illegal.

the thrill of producing elegant code[157] and the egoboo[158] from public recognition of one's efforts and skills has become not just the poster-child for free software but the only image many have of free software developers. However, a significant amount of free software development is done by people during work time in ordinary paid computing jobs and while a small proportion of this may be regarded as a "charitable contribution" by the organisation, it is more often the organisational version of "scratching one's own itch" than anything else. Other companies make free software pay sufficiently well to fund its development in consultancy, bespoke development, or support contracts.

Where software is developed in-house, many managers see the development and maintenance of this software as a costs centre only, and may seek to sell the software. For many reasons this is almost always a mistake, since developing software is a risky business venture that non-specialists usually fail at, and in addition the software may well represent (part of) the company's principal business advantage in it's primary field of operation. However, where the organisation in question is not a competitive commercial player, but a public sector or non-profit organisation, then the commercial advantage argument turns on its head. Since such organisations by their nature should (though for various political reasons they do not always see this) be interested in "raising the game" of others cooperatively. This is particularly

---

[157] or, in unfortunately too many cases code which the hacker feels is elegant but which is in fact uncommented unmaintainable spaghetti code.

[158] A term from science fiction fandom derived from "ego boost" to describe the pleasure gained from recognition for voluntary works. The prevalence of science fiction fans in early free software and online communities transferred the term (and provided some of the impetus behind community efforts as the driving force) to the free software community.

true in, for example, local government. In the UK, there has long been a tradition of sharing in-house software between authorities. While often not released beyond the "club" of UK local government, it is effectively a free software distribution model within a closed group of separate entities.

So, if one is working within the public/non-profit sector, there is a strong ethical argument that in-house software developments should be released under some form of communal access agreement. Indeed, if there is potential for a broader utilisation of such software beyond the relevant type of organisation, then a strong argument can be made that there is an ethical duty to release the software more widely. This argument has strengthened over the last fifteen years (such software products and sharing have existed long before then) with the development of effectively free systems for distribution of such software, for example via the Free Software Foundation's website or the Sourceforge site. As we discuss below, similar arguments can be made regarding the ethical argument for public sector organisations to use open data formats and to make some of the data they generate freely available in such formats.

Even for commercial companies with specific needs, developing in-house software under a free software license may be a sensible business decision. The adoption of a free software license approach allows the development team to incorporate elements of existing free software as part of their system. In-house systems teams need to be aware of the necessity to ensure that management, particularly management outside the technical department, are aware of the decision to use free software and need to keep good documentation on the origins of their code. In particular, it is incumbent upon IT staff to ensure that any suggestion of taking in-house developed systems and distributing them is provided with clear guidelines on the status of the inherited code and the implications of its license for any such distribution.

Commissioning Software

So far we have focussed on the license adopted by an in-house team developing software for internal use. However, many businesses use external software companies for their bespoke IT needs. Questions of licensing on the side of the commissioning company need careful consideration, which they often do not get. Many software houses will take a line on licensing that tries to tie in the commissioning company to the software house for future development work, and retains ownership of the commissioned work by the software house, for possible re-use in other projects, and even development into a package for general sale. Again, the commissioning company need to consider their needs in the negotiations, and need to consider the future carefully. Larger companies and public sector organisation, such as government departments, where they commission software from a third party will often, though not always, take the longer-term view and insist on some form of access to the source code. This can take a number of approaches, but can include transfer of ownership in the software, shared rights, source code escrow and code audit rights.

Transfer Of Ownership

A software house will typically demand higher payment for software developed with a transfer of ownership compared to software in which the company retains some or all of the rights. In fact, it may not be possible to transfer all of the rights to the commissioning organisation. The software house may have developed a set of libraries for various purposes some of which may already be used in previous projects, and the use of which for future projects may be absolutely necessary for their continued business. If the company has based some of their work on GPL or LGPL-licensed[159] precursors then they may not own the rights themselves to transfer. If a software house has the right skills to develop the software that the commissioning organisation needs, then it is likely that a full transfer of rights would not be sensible for the software house.

For the commissioning company, sole ownership is the equivalent of developing the software in-house, without needing to employ the software developers directly or on a long-term basis. It provides the benefit that the software can be later further developed in-house or by a third party, either for in-house use or for sale as a product, a strategy already dismissed above.

Shared Ownership

Shared ownership is a shorthand for a number of different ways of licensing the output of a piece of bespoke software. At one extreme the commissioning and developing organisations have equal but separate rights to the output of the project at the end. Each is free to develop the code further on their own or with other parties, and neither is constrained as to how these further development may be commercialised or used. At the other extreme, the commissioning company may have full access to the

---

[159] The GNU Lesser General Public License which allows other programs to call the relevant software as a separate library without the "share-alike" element of the GPL coming into play for the core program, only for any changes to the library.

source code and may use it and develop it for in-house use themselves or bring in contractors to perform such development, but may not sell the software to others nor pass on rights to third parties. The most common variant of this kind of arrangement lies in the middle, with pre-existing libraries etc from the software house being licensed for use by the commissioning company, perhaps including a time- or type-limited right of access to updates (such as updates to new versions of the operating system). The new software developed during the project is then subject to the common ownership of the commissioning and developing organisations as detailed above.

Source Code Escrow

Small software houses, like all small businesses, are in a precarious position. Without any ill intent on behalf of the owners and management of such companies, they frequently fold and their records, including their source code base, may be deleted or may end up in the hands of liquidators for whom their sole purpose is the realisation of the maximum funds from those assets in as short a time as possible. When one has commissioned software from a company which then goes under, the possibility is that both the original source code and/or the clear chain of ownership and associated rights, is lost. To defend against the negative impacts of this, but where the software house is unwilling to agree to a transfer of rights or shared ownership, the source code may be placed in "escrow": that is, it may be lodged with a trusted third party. A properly drawn up escrow agreement provides the commissioning company with both access to the source code and the equivalent rights of shared or transferred ownership if and only if the software house ceases trading, or possibly on violation of the contract. This ensures that the commissioning organisation is not left with a set of running object code but no way of fixing bugs or upgrading it. The trusted escrow company ensures that the original software house's rights are not voided until and unless they are out of business. Alternatively a contract providing the code to the commissioner but no rights to do anything, except possibly read it, can be agreed.

Code Audit Rights

The right to at least see the code of a commissioned piece of software, or even one which is available off-the-shelf, may be a requirement for certain types of business. Partly in response to concerns about deliberate backdoors placed in the dominant MS Windows operating system from various non-US governments, and in reaction to other pressures such as continuous accusations of monopoly leveraging from operating system to office software and back (see also the section of this paper on data formats) MS introduced the "Shared Source Initiative" which provides users of, and developers for, some of MS's products access to (part of) the source code of systems such as MS Windows and MS Office. Similar code auditing arrangements can be built into bespoke software development contracts, allowing representatives of the commissioner, usually including contractors, the right to check the source code for security holes, whether deliberate or inadvertent.

Open And Closed Development Environments

The output of a software project and the tools used to develop it have no technical requirement to share license structures. For example, the use for a number of years of a proprietary tool (BitKeeper) for controlling the source code of one of the most high profile free/open source programs (the Linux Kernel, a vital part of the GNU/Linux operating system) was very controversial. A license move by BitMover (the company who produces BitKeeper) in 2002 (Shaikh and Cornford, 2003) which tried to restrict use of BitKeeper and prevent developers of interoperable free software clients caused a significant disagreement amongst Linux developers.:

> *this License is not available to You if You...develop, produce, sell, and/or resell a product which contains substantially similar capabilities of the BitKeeper Software, or, in the reasonable opinion of BitMover, competes with the BitKeeper Software.*

The controversy was somewhat lessened when BitMover released their own free software (GPL v.2) client called bk-client to connect to BitKeeper repositories, although with limited capabilities. The controversy was re-ignited in 2005 when BitKeeper withdrew their support due to the efforts of some Linux developers to develop a full-featured client to connect to the BitKeeper servers. As a result even Linus Torvalds finally shifted his stance and engaged with other Linux developers to scratch their own source control itch and produced the free software system Git, a source control system designed for very large highly active projects.

Software Idea Patents

In 1979 the spreadsheet, often claimed as the killer app that ensured the success of the personal computer in ordinary office environments, was invented by Bricklin and Frankston. They did not attempt to file a patent, although they did consider it (a common myth is that patenting was not seriously considered by any programmers in the 70s). Bricklin describes their consideration on his personal website www.bricklin.com/patenting.htm:

> *Why didn't we patent the spreadsheet? Were we stupid?*
>
> *This is a very common question, since, by the late 1990's, software inventions were routinely patented. Today, it seems negligent to ignore patents. However, in 1979, when VisiCalc was shown to the public for the first time, patents for software inventions were infrequently granted. ... The publishers of VisiCalc ... retained a patent attorney who met with executives from Software Arts and Personal Software. The patent attorney explained to us the difficulty of obtaining a patent on software, and estimated a 10% chance of success, even using various techniques for hiding the fact that it was really software (such as proposing it as a machine). Given such advice, and the costs involved, we decided not to pursue a patent. ...*

By 1981 the situation had changed and software patents were being granted, although this growth of the patent system has been far from universal, and both the concept and its implementation in the US today remain controversial. The inclusion of software purely as software (and not as part of a larger invention) in the scope of the patent system outside the US has been one of the few failures of the US' commercial rules hegemony on so-called intellectual property rights (Drahos and Braithwaite, 2002) over the past thirty years. At present, despite various attempts by the

European Patent Office (EPO),[160] various major international firms who hold software patents in the US and would like to see them introduced worldwide, and the US trade representatives (Drahos and Braithwaite, 2002), so far the European Parliament has resisted attempts to introduce software patents. It is a perennial issue, however, and as of writing yet another discussion of European patent reform is underway, with various groups offering suggested wordings which they all claim will simply clarify matters and reinforce the status quo. Of course if one believes the allegations about the EPO then that status quo includes the granting of patents on software in the EU.

Stallman, and other free software exponents (including those on the open source side of the free/open source software philosophy) are vehemently opposed to software idea patents. As they point out, software is inherently abstract except where it controls a physical entity. Restricting the use of software concepts, it is claimed, undermines not only the whole ethos of free software[161] but would also undermine the rest of the software industry, producing such ridiculous barriers to entry that few others than today's software giants (MS, IBM, Oracle and Sun, all of whom hold vast cross-licensed patent portfolios) could ever afford to produce software. Critics of software idea patents also point to the fact that innovation in software has been, and

---

[160] It is alleged that as well as arguing on a policy-making level that software should be patentable in the EU as it is in the US, that the EPO has deliberately stretched the rules, or even broken them, in granting patents on software in an attempt to by pass the democratic decision-making of both the EU and Member States and effectively introduce software patents by grant rather than by statute.

[161] which has a license which cannot prevent distribution free of charge, and which therefore it would be difficult to find a way to provide the funding for patent license fees, let alone actually track distribution to assess per-user fees, the usual basis for a patent license

continues to be, incredibly healthy, even without the 'protection' supposedly offered by patents.

Communication Protocols

In defining communication protocols, there are a number of issues where the question can be classified as open or closed. These are: trust, interoperability and interface.

Trust In Communication Protocols

When the internet was first developed, certainty of delivery over uncertain physical connections was the principle at work in defining the protocols for communications. All computers attached to the network were trusted not to be the source of malicious communications. Thus when the protocols of the first individual to individual communications tool (email) was defined (RFC 821: SMTP [Simple Mail Transfer Protocol] in August 1982, Jon Postel) the system was designed to include the minimum overhead of information exchanged to enable transfer of the important content. As such, SMTP is a highly trusting and open protocol. A receiving machine trusts the data provided by the sending machine in terms of the origination of the data and by agreeing to forward messages to other recipient machines. As the internet expanded, this trusting approach could not be maintained and many systems closed down their willingness to forward messages to other recipients, unless the message comes from a known source. The volume of spam long ago reached the point that accepting mail from everywhere for forwarding is now not only discouraged but such open mail proxies are now routinely blocked from sending messages to most of the rest of the internet.

However, even now, reverse lookup of domain names compared to internet addresses are deemed too expensive, and more importantly too restrictive, the be implemented on many mail receipt systems. Email is, in many ways, the victim of its own success and constantly teetering on the brink of being overwhelmed by malicious use. Being a relatively light overhead (even now) communication protocol, and given the openness of its implementation even now, a large number of emails are program-to-person or even program-to-program communications. This provides one of a number of barriers to a wholesale replacement of the SMTP-based email system still in use today. The other barriers to its replacements include:

• The immense install base of email: every user online has at least one email account and more usually more than that. Some will run hundreds of accounts on different systems for different purposes.

• The criticality of email in person-person machine-person and machine-machine communications, and in particular the lack of knowledge of many systems people of exactly which protocols some of their software uses.

• The desire of governments to censor and monitor their citizens' communications produces in some circumstances a pressure from surveillance authorities to maintain a relatively-simple-to-eavesdrop-on service, while suggestions for authority-assigned trackable origination communication are resisted by citizens wary of the hidden agenda of surveillance cloaked in rhetoric about reducing malicious communications.

• The suggestions by some major players in the software industry to include proprietary formats, protocols and even patented methods in revised standards.

Communication Protocols And Interoperability

Communication is all about connecting people with each other, preferably when both of them wish to be connected. In a small network this can be handled by a variety of means, but the numeric rules of networks mean that beyond a relatively small size of network, scalability demands distribution of at least some authority. In addition interoperability becomes a major issue in any definition of a communication protocol. Take the example of instant messaging (IM). The concept of direct synchronous communication between users has been a feature of computer communications for a long time, the specification for IRC (internet Relay Chat: RFC 1459 May 1993 by Oikarinen and Reed) provided an open protocol by which users could log on to a server, select one or more channels of communication on that server, and converse with each other with a minimum of typing overhead. This open protocol served traditional internet user for many years and became one of the main communication alternatives, particularly for synchronous groups discussions, along with email and usenet. However, for the non-expert computer user AOL, Yahoo! and MS came to dominate this communication space.

The walled garden online service of America OnLine (AOL) introduced AIM (AOL Instant Messenger) in 1996. In 1997 they released a client for non-AOL internet users, but still only for AIM-registered users. In 1998 Yahoo! introduced their "Yahoo! Pager" system, including the familiar buddy list feature. Again, this system included a single log-on to the Yahoo! central server and one could only talk to other Yahoo! users. In 1999, MS released MSN Messenger as part of its MS Network (MSN) online offering. The original MSN Messenger client allowed users to interoperate with both AOL and Yahoo! IM systems, by providing their account details to the Messenger server. AOL, in particular, strongly criticised this practice (Hu and Junnarkar, 1999) citing security concerns but almost certainly more worried about their market share and the advertising revenue generated by the ad-supported standalone client as well as their own subscriber base. As we discuss below, AOL have also attempted to block other clients from connecting to their messaging server (claimed to be in an attempt to secure the system, but in reality almost certainly in defense of their revenue stream). After regular alterations to the server and message protocol made keeping changes up to date on the Messenger client impractical, MS abandoned attempts to technologically force interoperability of IM on AOL.

For many years after their launch, each of these systems stood alone. Unlike email which, despite efforts by many companies to appropriate it to their own private formats remains mainly open as discussed above, these separate systems that came to dominate the instant messaging were restricted to communication with other users on the same system. Many users maintained accounts on more than one, sometimes all three of these different systems. In 2006, MS and Yahoo! launched interoperability between their services. AOL, having been approached to join them, still maintains its standalone network.

Despite its open definition and multitude of servers and clients, the Jabber protocol remains a small player in the IM field. Newer services and systems such as Facebook and the iPhone continue to challenge AOL, MS and Yahoo!'s dominance, and internal instant messaging within organisations exist, often based on proprietary systems such as the venerable Lotus Notes internal communication suite.

Data Formats

Closely linked to the issue of communication protocols are the issue of data standards. Everything from SMS (text messages) limited to 56 characters up to the entire contents of the internet archive (formerly the wayback machine) which aims to preserve the contents and changes of the internet for the future, is stored in data formats of varying levels of abstraction and complexity. At base, digital data is simply a collection of ones and zeroes. It is the interpretation of that data that makes it meaningful and useful. In the early days of digital electronic computing, even the interpretation of the ordering of the ones and zeroes as a binary number was a source of format incompatibility, the "big-endian" versus "little-endian" approach. Even now, different computer hardware runs on different endianness due to a variety of historical and purpose-optimisation reasons beyond the scope of this article. Digital information is valueless if its format is not understood. This may be a deliberate part of a format, in fact, for example formatting information stored in marked meta-data tags may be ignored by devices or programs for whom that data is not relevant. This allows the possibility of backwards compatibility, an important element in data formats since for many applications a universal simultaneous upgrade can not be expected.

Data formats can be classified into three main categories: completely closed; published but proprietary-controlled; open standards. Examples of each of these formats include:

• Closed: The MS Office formats. Despite a badly flawed process allowing the specification of MS's XML-wrapped binary formats as a "standard" MS's Office formats, including .doc[x], .xls[x] etc. remain closed proprietary formats. Reverse engineering allows some interoperability of other software, such as OpenOffice.org, but this is far from perfect due to a lack of published specification for the meaning of some of the data.

• Published Proprietary: The original portable document format (PDF) developed and maintained by Adobe Inc. The full language specification was published by Adobe with the intent that programs other than those produced by Adobe can interpret and produce well-defined PDF files. Changes to the format were controlled by Adobe. PDF was later submitted to and approved by the ISO for formal standardisation.

• Open Standards: Despite early tag proliferation in browsers and web page editors, HTML (and related formats such as CSS, XHTML etc.) is now a standard developed and published by the World Wide Web Consortium (W3C). The drafts are developed by the W3C's HTML Working Group.

As described above with regards to software licensing, choices regarding data formats are often not given the attention they deserve in companies. In particular, companies choosing the software they will use to run their business often ignore the question of the format of the data they will hold. That data is crucial to their business, and a requirement to re-produce data from scratch due to lack of current software to interpret older data can be sufficient to devalue or even close a business. So, when considering software and data formats, businesses need to look both forward and backwards.

Data Formats For Software Houses

The meaning of a data format is open to anyone with access to the source code of a program that can interpret that data. While not the most efficient or simple of ways to provide access to a specification, it does the job. So, if a software house produces free software, or allows access to its source code under more or fewer conditions, then the data format specification is discoverable by those with that access.

If one is producing a proprietary program then one may still produce data formats following a published description (whether proprietary or open standard). Adobe's Acrobat and MS's Internet Explorer are both proprietary programs using published data formats.

Some customers, particularly public sector customers, have as part of their requirements that data produced by programs is stored in a specified format (see below on good practice for software users).

The reason for such requirements is the loss of data that has already occurred in many organisations, particularly large public organisations who invested early in the creation of large amounts of data. When a software or hardware company went out of business, unless the information technologists working for the organisation were sufficiently on the ball, the capacity to use existing software and hardware to produce data usable by the new systems could easily be lost (Digital preservation Coalition, undated).

It might seem an obvious benefit to allow a program to read in as many external formats as possible, whether proprietary (one's own or the reverse-engineered versions of other's), published or open standards. However, that brings one's own programs at least partly into the interoperability region. While reading data format X produced by program Y, a competitor to one's own offering Z, might provide a relatively simple transition route from program Y, it also allows for the possibility of companies maintaining program Y as a main option and using a very small number of licenses for Z where it capabilities are really needed.

Output formats are the trickier question, however. Vendor lock-in using proprietary formats has been the model of commercial software for almost three decades. The examples are numerous, with reverse-engineering of the basic data format battling against deliberate obfuscation of the meaning of the data by the original firm. As mentioned above, however, there are other options. In order to avoid losing control to a standards body, which may move slower than user needs, and may be subject to capture by one's opponents and used to prevent new capabilities from reaching the market in time to secure a solid commercial advantage, the Adobe option of publishing the data standard but retaining control of it, seems very sensible. Of course, this may still be captured by competitors branching the specification for their own purposes ("embrace, extend extinguish").

If one does not already have a lead in the marketplace, gaining it can be very difficult (Brynjolfsson and Kemerer, 1996). In this case, subscribing to standards bodies, gaining a seat at the table, and competing on the merits of one's programmers and vision of user needs, may be the better option. Certainly a revolt by users who may see the proprietary data format as a stranglehold on their own valuable data, and upgrade or maintenance costs that rise over time as a sufficient reason to bite the bullet and change platform (likely never to return) are a risk of the proprietary route.

Data Formats For Other Organisations

For organisations commissioning bespoke software/hardware or buying off-the-shelf materials, the choice of data formats which are in some sense open to them really should be the obvious choice. A good range of options for both input and output formats, and adherence to data format standards, are all good for their business. For the public sector in particular, this issue has been gaining some political traction for some time. The difficulty comes, as always, in the interoperability stakes when other organisations work with a closed standard. In the UK for example, some government contract documents have in the past been issued solely in MS Word format, and required the advanced scripting facilities of Word to be completed. Not running a professional edition of MS Word would bar an organisation from bidding for government tenders. Direct online submission systems are tending to move away from this desktop program model, but it can still cause problems. Digital access and preservation strategies need careful thought alongside interoperability questions, and the possibility of loss of everything must be weighed against the possible loss of richness in some data.

Community Or Customers

In these days of user generated content the phrase community is often bandied around by those running websites where the provider is solely an intermediary between users sharing their material. There are many analyses of the economics and social norms attaching to this idea (Surowiecki, 2004; Tapscott and Williams, 2006; Constitution Committee of the House of Lords, 2008). Here we consider the attitude of organisations to their main users. Those organisations can be etail (Amazon.com), information provision (Wikipedia.org, LATimes.com, YouTube.com), personal introductions between users (adultfriendfinder.com) social networking sites (Facebook.com, Mixi.jp) and many others. One of the things each of these sites has in common is that part of what they provide is generated by their users. In some cases, e.g. Wikipedia, it is all they provide. At the other end of the scale the LA Times online site is principally populated with the organisations own material with some commentary and discussion amongst users. From Amazons customer ratings and reviews to adultfriendfinders profiles to

Facebook and Mixis blogs, photos and friend lists, part of the buzz about these sites is their community rather than their customers. The software industry, combining their own and their users technical expertise, were one of the first types of business to see the advantage in helping their users to communicate with one another. However, this can be a double-edged sword. Whereas harnessing the Hacker Ethic (Himanen, 2001) of information sharing provided free user support by creating a resource of experienced users willing to share their knowledge with each other (and, crucially, with new users) it also creates a perfect opportunity for unhappy users to report their woes to other users and potential users. Of course, these days most people have ample other places to air their poor customer experiences, but few have the fame of Eugene Volokh (Solove, 2007, p.93) and hence a blog post by most will barely attract any significant attention, but if its more than a few complaining bitterly on an official site, then the organisation can have real problems. When posted to an organisation-owned community site, such comments can, perhaps, be removed, but the very act of creating a forum where users provide most of the content is that they feel that they gain some, if not all, of the expected free speech rights of public places (Sunstein, 2002, Klein, 2000) and hard censorship on such sites will tend to undermine their benefits in general while possibly driving away existing customers more unhappy with the censorship than because of the original failings.

Where the content of a site is created principally by the users, and the organisation provides a structure in which to hold that content, questions of ownership come into play. The rhetoric of publishers has long been that copyright derives from the brilliant acts of creation performed by the artist (writer, composer, musician) and that the long, strong and wide protection is needed to provide the deserving creator with the just benefits. of course, the fact that the middlemen have been taking the lion's share of all the income is never mentioned. This case becomes even more difficult when sites such as YouTube are considered. Created in 2005, YouTube quickly gathered a huge base of video clips from users, free for other users to view. These clips included home videos (everything from the funny antics of a cat to political diatribes), film student shorts and extracts from commercial material. Even in the early days the commercial content caused some difficulties for the site operators, with complaints from music recording companies, film companies and television production companies. When Google acquired YouTube for in 2006 these companies redoubled their efforts to either shut YouTube down, or at the very least acquire a share in its profits. This raises an interesting question, however, of what Google actually bought, and from whom. The terms and conditions of the YouTube site are that uploaders provide an irrevocable license for YouTube to do pretty much everything they want with the material thus uploaded. In typical middleman style this included selling the entire site to Google for $1.65b without ever paying existing users a cent for their content. Under various pressures, Google introduced a profit sharing plan in 2007 to enable uploaders of very popular videos to receive some of the advertising income that funds the service. It remains one of the few user-generated content sites to have any form of plan no such site to my knowledge has shared an IPO or massive sale proceeds with their users.

The Anti-Malware Prisoners' Dilemma

Anti-virus software has been around for a long time. Viri and other forms of malware have been circulating since the early days of the mini computer and the forerunner of the internet. Anti-virus and related security software has become big business. Major community efforts are also put into identifying both vulnerabilities and threats. CERTs (computer emergency readiness/response teams) exist in all the developed countries and a number of others, with local teams also in existence. The threat and risks are seen as so important that the main US-CERT is now part of the Department of Homeland Security.

Like much else in the world of security, most people are not very good at dealing with it. Many do not install any significant protections until they have been badly damaged at least once, and sometimes a number of times, by malware attacks. Given the potential for indirect harm from many modern malware, where the machine in question is merely hijacked (turned into a zombie) and its network connection used for the sending of spam, participation of distributed denial of service attacks or for use in cracking high-value machines, this is an unfortunate position. It does mean, however, that advertising and selling security software is difficult. Competition in this marketplace is therefore quite fierce. This is one area, however, where competition probably does not produce the optimum outcome. The reason for this is that there are two major parts to anti-malware programs. The first is an overseer program that monitors what is going on in the operating system and looks for other pieces of software whose actions are out of the ordinary (accessing many different types of file, adding the same code to each, for example). The second is a set of recognition signatures for identified malware and unpatched vulnerabilities in programs. If a piece of malware appears on the computer via any route the easiest, quickest and most effective way for the anti-malware program to identify it is with a software signature: some element(s) of the virus' code identified as unchanging between minor variations.

In an ideal world these virus signatures would be freely shared between anti-malware companies and given away free to users. However, identification of these signatures is a time-consuming job and while some of this is done by volunteers or CERT team members, much of it is done by paid employees of the anti-malware company. While free sharing of the signature files would probably make all computers safer from infection, such sharing would also, particularly if not reciprocated, reduce the competitiveness of a company's software in the security marketplace. If Company A shares its identified signatures with everyone else, then the software from all companies will detect the viri that Company A's software does, plus the ones they have separately identified but not shared. In addition, it is likely that churn[162] in the marketplace is at least partly driven by failure of the existing software to prevent infection. So, sharing virus signatures can reduce churn, and thus reduce the ability of companies offering better programs to gain customers during the churn. So, instead of cooperating, the anti-malware companies defect and everyone loses out.

Conclusions

When software is produced by public or non-profit organisations, the mode of operation should almost certainly be some form of free software license. Not only does this allow their programmers free reign to build on existing free software and not re-invent the wheel, but by explicitly collaborating with other public/non-profit organisations with similar problems to solve, a cooperative effort can yield quicker and sturdier results than a solo effort in each organisation. The (ideally) lack of any form of

---

[162] That is, customers shifting from one product to another.

competition among public and non-profit organisations generally removes any doubts that internal developments should be released in this way.

Similarly to public and non-profit organisations, commercial organisations should consider building on existing free software projects, either forking them to develop into serving their own needs or contributing to the general development of a particular project. Few pieces of software developed for in-house use are ever successfully commercialised and building internal tools on free software can prevent managers from following this dangerous path.

As has been shown by a number off companies, some of them major players (IBM, RedHat, Sun) developing free software can provide valuable income. Instead of competing with other companies for a locked-in client base paying for regular upgrades, maintenance and support of a proprietary program, competing for business offering a specific service can lead to a healthier long-term business. Certainly the ethical values of the ACM and BCS where the customer, society, the developers and the business are all seen as stakeholders in the information infrastructure, free software is much more compatible with these values. The use of free software as a company's offering encourages it to regard its highly skilled development staff as its most valuable resource, and not as a cost base whose benefits and salaries should be kept down at all costs. Treating one's knowledge workers as the core of the business fits well with the shift to the knowledge economy described by so many including Castells (1996, 1997, 2000). Regarding one's knowledge workers as less important than the managers and sales staff is the stuff of Dilbert's world and can often be the downfall of a company, in the long if not the short term.

The arguments against patents generally have been made many times for both philosophical (Jefferson, 1907, pp.326–338, Vol. XIII, Letter to Isaac McPherson) and practical (Drahos and Braithwaite, 2002) reasons. The particular case against restrictions on software are compelling:

- Without software patenting, the software industry in Europe has not imploded nor suffered from a lack of investment.

- The level of innovation in software is very high and as patents are supposed to promote innovation by rewarding it. Since the innovation exists patents are unnecessary.

- Few software patents issued in the US have ever been successfully defended against charges of lack of novelty, obviousness (to a relevant practitioner), or published prior art.

- If the idea of the spreadsheet had been patented in 1979, the base idea would only have dropped out of patenting in 1999. The world of computing in 1999 and that of 1979 were so radically different it is hard to see this as a sensible term.

- The return on investment period for software is so variable, depending on too many factors, for a sensible term to be valid across software.

- Software is so abstract, malleable and variable that the only beneficiaries in the long run are likely to be lawyers.

- Even for large software concerns, the risks in developing any new code would be substantial whereas the rewards are uncertain.

Publishing the details of communication protocols usually benefits the developers of the original system using the protocol because the network multiplication factor outweighs the detriments of increased competition. Sometimes a first mover can gain and maintain a closed protocol system, but they run the risk of losing their market share very quickly (e.g. the closed protocols of Friendster, one of the early mass appeal social networking sites lost out to the similarly closed protocols of Facebook, although the closed protocol of AIM still puts AOL at the top of the IM market). Protocols themselves should not be too open or trusting of information coming in. The early days of trusting everyone on the network are long gone and there is too much pollution in the information stream for open, trusting protocols.

Where feasible, the users of software (whether that be off-the-shelf or bespoke) always benefit from known formats. The differences between published but owned formats and true standards are complicated and often depend on the particular type of document, its purposes and user base. Proprietary formats, like closed protocols, can produce customer lock-in and dominant market share, but reverse-engineering is likely to cause an arms race and some large customers such as governments may well have the power to demand, or even force, the opening of a format specification.

Members of a community are more likely to be forgiving of failings than pure customers, and to have some sort of emotional investment in the software or service they are using. However, members of a community also have greater expectations of responsiveness and other elements of human rights come in to play. The ACM and BCS code of ethics, with their stress on balancing stakeholder interests including those of customers should push computing professionals down the road of community-building. Provided you treat your customers well and don't set out to exploit them. the benefits can far outweigh the downsides, particularly in user to user support.

The Costs And Benefits Of Openness

Being open has its risks, particularly for things like communication protocols, where trusting protocols are now almost always abused. By adopting an open approach in general, businesses can develop a more balanced approach to their activities, being paid for what they do and will do, rather than trying to be paid for what they have already done. Higher risks may bring higher rewards in the long run, but they also may not. If long term value is your goal, a more open approach can produce a more efficient economy, which can have broad benefits. In particular, the use of free software licenses, open formats and building communities should help us to develop a more robust software infrastructure. Competition based on continuing ability to meet user needs is healthier than one based on long-term lock-in, see-saw (teeter-totter) economics (Hunt, 2000) and customer exploitation. Arguments about universal interoperability are often used by companies such as Microsoft to explain their effective-monopoly position as good for the consumer. Open formats, clear distinctions between infrastructure, utility and productivity applications and competition in the marketplace reduce barriers to entry, and force companies to maintain the quality of their offerings far more than a captive market. Excess profits in the software industry syphon money from elsewhere in the economy and claims that this is healthy are an example of the Broken Window Fallacy (Bastiat, 1850). Monopolies can also be brittle in a number of ways, including security risks associated with monocultures (if almost everyone runs a particular piece of software then any vulnerability in that software makes it more attractive to attackers and more devastating when an attack occurs), and the problem of one monopoly replacing another, whereby the previous monopolist may swiftly find themselves bankrupt.

References

1. Bastiat, F. (1850). What is Seen and What is Not Seen. In (Bastiat, 1964). Original essay published in 1850; available online.

2. Bastiat, F. (1964). Selected Essays on Political Economy. Van Nostrand, Princeton, NJ.

3. Brynjolfsson, E. and Kemerer, C. F. (1996). network externalities in microcomputer software: An econometric analysis of the spreadsheet market. Management Science, 42(12):1627–1647. www.katzis.org/wiki/images/9/9f/ Brynjolfsson_1996.pdf.

4. Castells, M. (1996). The Rise of the Network Society. Number 1 in The Information Age. Blackwell, Chichester.

5. Castells, M. (1997). The Power of Identity. Number 2 in The Information Age. Blackwell, Chichester.

6. Castells, M. (2000). End of Millennium. Number 3 in The Information Age. Blackwell, Chichester.

7. Chandler, J. A. (2008). Contracting insecurity: Software license terms that undermine cybersecurity. In [Matwyshyn, 2008], pages 159–201.

8. Constitution Committee of the House of Lords (2008). Second Report; Surveillance; Citizens and the State. www.publications.parliament.uk/pa/ld200809/ldselect/ldconst/ 18/1802.htm.

9. Digital Preservation Coalition. Handbook of preservation management of digital materials. www.dpconline.org/graphics/handbook/.

10. Drahos, P. and Braithwaite, J. (2002). Information Feudalism. Earthscan.

11. Feller, J., Fitzgerald, B., Hissam, S., and Lakhani, K., editors (2003). Taking Stock of the Bazaar: Proceedings of the 3rd Workshop on Open Source Software Engineering. Available online as opensource.ucc.ie/icse2003/.

12. Gates III, W. H. (1976). An open letter to hobbyists. www.blinkenlights.com/classiccmp/gateswhine.html.

13. Himanen, P. (2001). The Hacker Ethic and the Spirit of the Information Age. Vintage, New York, NY. Prologue by Linus Torvalds, epilogue by Manuel Castells.

14. Hu, J. and Junnarkar, S. (1999). AOL blocks Microsoft Net messaging. CNet News. news.cnet.com/2100-1023-228960.html.

15. Hunt, S. (2000). A general theory of competition: Resources, competences, productivity, economic growth. Sage, Thousan Oaks, CA.

16. Jefferson, T. (1907). Writings of Thomas Jefferson. The Thomas Jefferson Memorial Association.

17. Klien, N. (2000). No Logo. Picador, New York, NY.

18. Levy, S. (2001). Hackers: Heroes of the Computer Revolution. Penguin, London.

19. Loren, L. P. (2004). Slaying the Leather-Winged Demons in the Night: Reforming Copyright Owner Contracting with Clickwrap Misuse. Ohio Northern University law Review, 30(3):495–536.

20. Matwyshyn, A., editor (2008). Harboring Data: Information Security, Law, and the Corporation. Stanford Law Books, Stanford, CA.

21. May, C. (2003). Digital rights management and the breakdown of social norms. First Monday, 8(11).

22. Raymond, E. S. (2001). The Cathedral and the Bazaar. O'Reilly. Available online.

23. Shaikh, M. and Cornford, T. (2003). Version Management Tools: CVS to BK in the Linux Kernel. In Feller et al., 2003, pages 127–132. Available online as opensource.ucc.ie/ icse2003/.

24. Shirky, C. (2008). Here Comes Everybody. Allen Lane, London.

25. Solove, D. J. (2007). The Future of Reputation. Yale University Press, New Haven, CT.

26. Stefik, M. (1997). Shifting the possible: How trusted systems and digital property rights challenge use to rethink

digital publishing. Berkeley Technology Law Journal, 12(1): 137–160.

27. Sunstein, C. R. (2002). Republic.com. Princeton University Press, Princeton, NJ. Second edition also available: Republic.com 2.0, 2007.

28. Surowiecki, J. (2004). The Wisdom of Crowds. Doubleday, New York, NY.

29. Tapscott, D. and Williams, A. D. (2006). Wikinomics. Portfolio, New York, NY.

30. Williams, S. (2002). Free as in Freedom; Richard Stallman's Crusade for Free Software. O'Reilly, Sebastapol, CA.

Andrew Adams is Deputy Director of the Centre for Business Information Ethics and Professor at the Graduate School of Business Administration, Meiji University. His research interests are in the social impact of computer and communication technology and related legislation and regulation. He has a PhD in Computer Science from the University of St Andrews and an LLM (Masters) in Law from the University of Reading. He is a founding member of the UK's Open Rights Group. He co-authored Pandora's Box: Social and Professional Issues of the Information Age, available from Wiley. He has published papers on issues of copyright, privacy, ubiquitous computing in healthcare and other topics.

Blurring the Line between Creator and Consumer

By Andrew Katz

We are reaching the end of a great historical experiment. Printing (starting with Gutenberg-style presses, and leading to huge industrial Heidelberg printing machines), radio broadcasting, records (shellac 78s and vinyl), CDs, cinema, television, DVDs and Blu-Rays were the technological backdrop for this experiment. All are (or were) media based on the principle of one-to-many distribution. To understand how this experiment was initiated, and how it is reaching its end, we need to understand a little of the nature of the businesses involved in these activities, and how the law enabled them to attain, and retain, that nature.

The one-to-many broadcast distribution model distorted our perception of creativity. A key characteristic of one-to-many distribution is the role of the gatekeeper: the corporation which decides what we, the public, get to read, hear, watch or listen to. The roles of creator and consumer are starkly defined and contrasted. The public becomes used to the idea of passive consumption, and creativity, in those areas covered by copyright becomes increasingly marginalised: perceived as capable of flourishing only through the patronage of the movie studios, the record companies or the TV stations.

The industrial technology behind printing, broadcasting and vinyl duplication is expensive. Copyright law grants a monopoly which enables the distributors of content to invest in the capital infrastructure required for its packaging and distribution. These are the businesses which grew fat on the monopolies so granted, and they succeeded in convincing the public that it was the corporations' role to provide, and the public's role to pay and consume.

The original social approach to creativity did not become extinct as the dominant producer/consumer mode become established, even for media (like music, for example) where it applied. Andrew Douglas's excellent film *Searching for the Wrong-Eyed Jesus* shows that a visitor to the late 20th century Appalachians of the American South, may well be asked "What instrument do you play?". If the visitor answers "I don't", the questioner will go on to say "Ok, so you must sing".

Steven Johnson, in *Where Good Ideas Come From* makes the convincing case, based on a mass of evidence, that this social mode is more effective at maximising creativity that relying on lone inventors and creators sitting in their garrets and sheds. Lone creators make a good central figure in a compelling narrative (which is one reason why this meme is so popular). However, examining the truth behind the narrative often reveals that any creative work has much broader parentage than the story suggests. James Boyle in *The Public Domain* reveals the story behind the Ray Charles song *I Got a Woman*, tracing it backwards to Gospel roots, and forwards to the YouTube mashup *George Bush Doesn't Care About Black People,* which sprung to prominence in the aftermath of hurricane Katrina. To be sure, companies sometimes tried to foster a social model *within* the organisation, but as Johnson points out, the benefits of social creation increase very dramatically with the size of the pool of participants, due to network effects (Metcalfe's law – the number of connections increases with the square of the number of participants): until company silos are able to combine, the beneficial effects are relatively small.

The internet proved hugely disruptive. The sharing and social nature of Web 2.0 has enabled the rediscovery of the natural, human, social mode of creative endeavour. The social side of the internet is dominated by individuals acting in their private capacity, outside the scope of businesses. Businesses, initially wary of losing control over the activities of their staff, and which regarded internet social activities as, at best, time wasting, and, at worst, providing the potential to leak the company's "valuable intellectual property", were often slow to see the benefits of social interaction in terms of benefits to their creativity. However, as they have seen the benefits accrue to their competitors, they are starting to embrace a more open mode of business.

A return to the social mode is not without setbacks. The internet radically lowered the barrier to entry for collaborative participation, and consequently increased the number of potential contacts that an entrant can make. This immensely powerful engine of creativity is also subject to a brake: the effect of unfit-for-purpose copyright laws.

The copyright laws of the broadcast era do more to assist the incumbent gatekeepers (the film companies, music companies and so-on) than to promote the social mode of collaboration. A side-effect of the digital world is that almost every form of digital interaction involves copying of some sort. Whereas copyright law has nothing to say about sharing a book with a friend by lending it to her, in the digital realm, lending her a digital copy of *Nineteen Eighty-Four* to read on her e-book reader or computer involves and of copying which can potentially violate copyright law.

The broadcast-model gatekeepers have relied on this unintended side-effect of copyright law to their advantage, taking action against private individuals who had no intention of monetary gain, including mash-up artists, home video enthusiasts and slash fiction authors.

Incumbent rights-holders, fearful of losing their profitable monopoly-based businesses, have sought to extend their rights ever further, by (frequently successfully lobbying) governments to legislate for new and increased intellectual property rights, far beyond their original purpose and intention.

To put the issue in context, it is necessary to ask the fundamental question: "What is copyright for?"

Thomas Jefferson was one of the most lucid writers on the topic. He understood well the unique nature of knowledge:

"If nature has made any one thing less susceptible than all others of exclusive property, it is the action of the thinking power called an idea, which an individual may exclusively possess as long as he keeps it to himself; but the moment it is divulged, it forces itself into the possession of every one, and the receiver cannot dispossess himself of it. Its peculiar character, too, is that no one possesses the less, because every other possesses the whole of it. He who receives an idea from me, receives instruction himself without lessening mine; as he who lights his taper at mine, receives light without darkening me. That ideas should freely spread from one to another over the globe, for the moral and mutual instruction of man, and improvement of his condition, seems to have been peculiarly and benevolently designed by nature, when she made them, like fire, expansible over all space, without lessening their density in any point, and like the air in which we breathe, move, and have our physical being, incapable of confinement or exclusive appropriation. Inventions then cannot, in nature, be a subject of property."

But Jefferson conceded that creative people should be given a limited right of exclusive control over their creations. Even though a monopoly is inherently a bad thing (as was recognised in the late 18th century just as it is today), nonetheless, a monopoly of control, in the form of copyright or a patent, was the most convenient way of enabling the creators to be remunerated for their work. And once the monopoly expired the, idea would be freely available for all and become part of the common heritage of mankind, to be used without restriction by anyone. The necessary (but limited) monopoly includes "copyright", and the principle that the restrictions should be the minimum possible to achieve that aim should be copyright's golden rule.

The golden rule has been repeatedly ignored. The scope of protection has steadily increased over the last three hundred years, to the extent that, in Europe, the protection granted to the author of a novel, for example, lasts for seventy years after his or her death.

What isn't restricted by intellectual property is called "the public domain".

Commentators have become increasingly strident that the public domain is a public good (an idea with which Jefferson would have agreed). In the same way that a common land is open to all to graze their animals, the public domain has been described as a commons of knowledge, where potentially anyone can graze on the intellectual creations of others. The public domain has one crucial difference from a commons in the tangible world: a meadow open to all can easily be over-grazed and ruined, so that it becomes of use to no one (the so-called "tragedy of the commons"). It is impossible to exhaust the commons of knowledge and ideas.

The modern "tragedy of the commons" is that, just as the internet makes it easier to pass ideas and knowledge from one person to another (for "the moral and mutual instruction of man, and improvement of his condition") it seems that legislation and the more extreme activities of the rights holders are making it more difficult for those ideas and knowledge to enter the commons in the first place. This is because the term of intellectual property is forever extending (will the early Mickey Mouse films ever enter the public domain?), and so is its scope (for example, the patenting of genes or plants).

Increasingly, people are becoming aware of the value of the commons, and are seeking to protect it. At the same time, we are becoming aware that the monopoly granted by intellectual property laws is a blunt instrument, and that people are prepared to create for reasons other than the expectation of payment for the use of their creation.

Copyright law does not always have to work against the commons.

In the late 1980s, Richard Stallman, a computer programmer, realised that copyright law could be turned inside out to create a commons of computer software. The method he proposed was simple, but brilliant:

Software is protected by copyright. The existing software business model involved granting customers permission (the licence) to use a specific piece of software. This licence was conditional on the customer not only paying the software publisher fee, but also adhering to a number of other restrictions (such as only using the software on one computer, for example). Why not, Stallman reasoned, make it a condition of the licence, that if you took his software and passed it on (which he was happy for people to do), then they had to pass it on, together with any changes they made, under the same licence? He called this sort of software "free software": once a piece of software has been released under this sort of licence, it can be passed on freely to other people, with only one restriction: that if they pass it on, in turn, they must also ensure the people they pass it on in a way that guarantees and honours that freedom.

In time, he reasoned, more and more software would be released under this licence, and a commons of freely available software would flourish.

In the two decades since the most widely used version of the licence (called the GNU General Public License version 2 – called the GPL) was issued it has become the most commonly used software licence. It is the licence at the core of Linux, the computer operating system which powers Google. Amazon, Facebook and which enabled Red Hat to generate revenue in excess of $1.5Bn in financial year 2013-14.

The GPL software commons not only exists: by any measure it is an overwhelming success, whether it is in terms of number of participants creating software for it; whether it is the number of items of GPL software in use; whether it is in the environments in which GPL software can be found (from running over 90% of the worlds 100 most powerful computers, to mobile phones and in-car entertainment systems); whether it is at the core of the business offerings of businesses like IBM and Red Hat.

The success of free software is not just down to the GPL. The GPL extracts a price for using the commons. To analogise possibly too far, a landowner adjoining the GPL commons who wants to use it also has to add his own land to the commons (although, remember that this is the magical land of ideas which cannot be ruined by over-grazing). This will have the effect of increasing the size of the commons as more and more adjoining landowners want to make use of the commons and donate their own land in the process. But many of them may not want to join this scheme: either because they don't want to add their own land to the commons, or because they have already pledged their land to another commons.

Is it possible to generate a commons of ideas without forcing participants to pay the price of entry: that they add their own adjoining land to the commons? Is the compulsion of the GPL necessary, or is the social and community dynamic powerful enough to allow a similar commons of ideas to spring up on its own?

The software industry has given us several outstanding examples of this. Apache, the most popular web server software in the world (and used by many of the busiest web sites) is issued under a licence which doesn't ask users to pay the GPL price. Anyone can take the Apache code, and modify it and combine it with their other software, and release it without having to release any sources to anyone else. In contrast to the GPL, there is no compulsion to add your software to the Apache commons if you build on Apache software and distribute your developments, but many people choose to contribute back without this compulsion. FreeBSD, to take another example, is an operating system with similarities to GNU/Linux which is licensed under a very liberal licence allowing its use, amendment and distribution without the *requirement* to contribute improvements back: nonetheless, many people *choose* to do so.

The GPL tackles an issue called the *free rider* problem. Because BSD does not compel people to contribute back to the commons, those who take advantage without contributing back are called *free riders*. The question is whether free riders really are a problem (as the GPL band would maintain), or they are (as the BSD band would maintain) at worst a cost-free irritant, or at best, a cadre of people who will eventually see the light and start to contribute, once they recognise the benefits.

Supporters of both the GPL and BSD models of licensing have similar aims: the production of a software commons which will enable the social mode of creativity to flourish.

While the BSD model could subsist in the absence of copyright, GPL relies (perhaps ironically) on copyright law to enforce its compulsion to share. It still remains an open question as to whether the better model is to use licensing to compel people to participate in the software commons, and reduce the free rider problem (as with GPL), or whether voluntary engagement will result in a more active community (as with Apache). As we will see below, designers working outside the digital domain will rarely have the ability to choose a GPL-style option.

The undoubted success of free and open source software (Gartner confidently states that all businesses today use at least some free software in their systems. The Linux Foundation estimated that free software underpinned a $50 billion economy in 2011) means that this model has been considered for its applicability in other contexts. Can designers in other fields benefit from this model?

One of the most prominent of these has been the Creative Commons movement. Founded in 2001, Creative Commons has written a suite of licences which were inspired by the GNU GPL, but which are intended for use in relation to a broad range of media, including music, literature, images and movies. The licences are drafted to be simple to understand and are modular, in that the rights owner can choose from a selection of options. The *attribution* option requires that anyone making use of the work makes fair attribution to the author; the *share alike* option is akin to the GPL, in that if a licensee takes the work and redistributes it (whether amended or not), then the redistribution needs to be on the same form of licence; the *no derivatives* option means that work may be passed on freely, but not modified, and the *non commercial* option means that the work can only be used and distributed in a non-commercial context.

There are now millions of different works available under on of the various creative commons licences: Flickr is just one search engine which has enabled Creative Commons licensing as a search option. There are, at the time of writing (2014), over 300,000,000 Creative Commons licensed images available for use on Flickr alone (up from just under 200,000,000 in 2010, when the first version of this article was written). Similar sites provide music and literary works under a Creative Commons licence.

The Creative Commons provides designers and other creatives operating within the digital domain the legal infrastructure to adopt this model. There is also an effective choice as to whether an appropriate model is GPL-style share-alike, or BSD style. Where designers' work moves into the physical world, all is not so straightforward.

The movement of hardware design into the commons has been difficult. The issues are fundamentally:

1. In the digital world, the creator has the choice of whether a GPL- or BSD- model is appropriate. This choice does not translate well to the analogue world.

2. Digital works are relatively easy to create and test on low-cost equipment. Analogue works are more difficult to create, test and copy, and this creates barrier-to-entry problems.

3. Digital goods are easy to transport. Analogue ones frequently aren't. This creates a barrier to the communication necessary to get the most benefit out of network effects.

The barrier to entry for any participant in a digital project is remarkably low. A low-cost computer and basic internet access are all that is required to have a system capable of running the (free) GNU/Linux operating system and accessing project hosting sites like github.com (which is free of charge to public projects).

A vast range of tools required to develop software (such as GCC – the GNU Compiler Collection) is also available as free software. Copying purely digital works is trivially easy. Physical objects are a different matter.

Hardware development is likely to require more intensive investment in equipment (including premises), not just for development, but for testing. Electronic digital hardware is probably closest to software in terms of low barrier to entry: for example, the open-source Arduino micro-controller project enables an experimenter to get started with as little as $30 for a basic USB controller board (or less, if the experimenter is prepared to build the board). Arduino's schematics, board layouts and prototyping software are all open source. However, Arduino-like projects represent the lowest barrier to entry in the hardware world.

The Arduino-style project is essentially a hybrid of the analogue and the digital domains. Prototyping software makes it possible to develop Arduino-based hardware in the digital domain, where it retains all the characteristics of the digital world: ease of copying, the ability to upload prototypes to fellow-contributors for commentary, assistance and showing off. These are characteristics which enable network effects, and which make the open source model so powerful. It is only when the project is implemented as a physical circuit board that these characteristics are lost.

The analogue world is not always so simple. One of the most ambitious open source projects is the 40 Fires/Riversimple hydrogen car project, which has developed a small urban car (the Hyrban) powered by hydrogen, using a fuel cell/electric drivetrain. Elements of the design (for example power control software, or the dashboard user interface) can be developed largely in the digital domain, but the development of motors, brakes, the body shell and so-on are strictly analogue only, and not only present a large barrier-to-entry for interested tinkerers, but also tend to restrict the ability to participate in the development community: a necessity if network effects are to work. It is, clearly, difficult to upload a car to a development site and say "can you tell me why the windscreen leaks?".

Another significant issue is the lack of design software at a low cost. Software developers have access to high quality tools like development environments and tools available for free under free software licences. There is no similar suite of CAD software, and proprietary CAD software is notoriously expensive. The barrier to entry is raised once again.

Many of these issues are surmountable, in time. Ever-improving simulation software means that more and more testing and prototyping can be undertaken in the digital domain. The introduction of 3-d printers, such as the RepRap, means that printing physical objects, such as gears, for example, out a variety of plastics, is becoming increasingly affordable and feasible. The lack of suitable CAD software is being addressed by a number of projects.

For designers, progress in open source tools, increased connectivity and so-on makes the establishment of open-source communities ever more feasible. The legal issues are, however, not so straightforward.

So far, we have concentrated on copyright issues. Other forms of intellectual property pose, in some ways, greater challenges. Copyright protects the expression of an idea. Retaining the same idea, but recasting the expression of it in a different form does not infringe the copyright. The story of two people from warring tribes meeting, falling and love, and dying in tragic circumstances can be told in a myriad different ways, each with their own independent copyright, and without infringing anyone else's copyright. This has two practical consequences. The first is that if a creator creates something which he or she has not copied from something else, then the creator will not be in breach of copyright, even if their creation turns out to be very similar, or even identical, to someone else's. The second is that if a component of something is found to be infringing copyright, it is possible to rewrite it by recasting the same idea in a different expression.

Copyright also has the advantage of being (reasonably well) harmonised worldwide, and has also proved amenable to hacking (by Richard Stallman) so that it can be used to guarantee freedom in the code it covers.

There are other forms of intellectual property protection, and, for designers, these are more problematic.

This issue is linked to the distinction between the analogue and digital domains. Designs will almost invariably start with some sort of drawing or description. This will be protected as a literary or artistic work by copyright. Often, this material will be digital in nature. At this point, it's similar to software. Licensing options include the suite of Creative Commons licences. Once an item is created in the physical world, a different set of legal considerations applies.

The most obvious is design right. Unfortunately, design right is complex and uncoordinated. There are many different types of design right. In the UK, for example, there are four separate design right regimes operating simultaneously, covering (depending on the right in question) aspects such as shape, texture, colour, materials used, contours and ornamentation. Registered designs are in many ways similar to patents (and are sometimes called petty patents or design patents). Infringement can be unintentional, and independent creation is irrelevant. Unregistered designs are more in the nature of copyrights, and are capable of infringement only where copying has taken place. The very fact that registration is required (in the case of registered design rights, clearly), itself provides a barrier to entry for collaborative projects: whereas copyright arises automatically and without the necessity of registration, who will pay for the preparation of a design registration, and who will make the application and maintain it?

Patents provide a particular problem for both programmers and designers, as they can impinge on both the digital realm and the analogue realm. Patents are a protection on the idea itself. However that idea is expressed, the patent will be infringed. Independent invention does not excuse patent infringement. The only way to be sure that an invention does not infringe a patent is to do an exhaustive check in patent offices worldwide: something that is very rarely done (the expense is enormous and creates a vast barrier to entry for small businesses, and US law in particular applies a positive disincentive to search: if a search is undertaken, then the searcher can be deemed to have knowingly infringed a patent – even if their reasonable determination was that the patent was not infringed – and will be liable to triple damages as a consequence).

Pressure groups are lobbying worldwide for a reform of the patent system and process, but at present it is clear that the system benefits incumbent large companies with an existing patent portfolio.

The upshot of the intellectual property issues is that whereas those operating wholly in the digital domain (which includes programmers, but which can also extend to digital creatives such as filmmakers, novelists or graphic designers) have the ability to choose whether they prefer the GPL model to the BSD model, for a number of reasons, the BSD model is often a more viable option in the hardware, analogue world. The main reasons are, briefly, that (1) copyright, being largely universal, automatic, unregistered and long-lasting, is better suited to the development of a copyleft model that other forms of intellectual property; and (2) that the difference in cost between copying something and reverse engineering (which is vast in digital world, but much smaller in the analogue world), makes the copyleft a less compelling point).

These reasons probably need some explanation.

For a GPL-model to apply to hardware designs, to be effective, it would need to impinge on the ideas underlying the design (meaning patents), or on the visual characteristics of the design (meaning design rights). A GPL-style model based on patents would likely fail (at least when any of the participants are not large corporations) because of the cost, complexity, and time involved in applying for the patents (and the necessity to keep the invention secret prior to its publication as part of the application process squares badly with the open source ethos). If the model were based on design rights, this would fail in relation to registered design rights, for the same reasons as for patents, and for unregistered design rights would be unlikely to work because the scope and length of protection would be too short, and because the rights are insufficiently universal (although there is some scope for a limited GPL-style model in relation to unregistered design rights).

There is also an economic argument why a GPL model may cause problems in the field of hardware. The reasoning is as follows: the digital world makes things extremely easy to copy. Imagine a programmer wants to create some software based on a program with similar functionality to a word processor, for example, released under the GPL. The options are (1) take the original GPL program, modify it, and release the result under the GPL; or (2) take the GPL program, reverse engineer it, and rewrite a whole new program from scratch, which will be unencumbered by copyright restrictions. The difference in the amount of work involved in the two scenarios is vast, and any programmer is likely to consider very seriously adopting the easier, cheaper and quicker option (1), where the "cost" is out-licensing under the GPL. However, even if there were a functioning mechanism for applying share-alike to, for example, a mechanical assembly, in this case, an engineer wishing to reproduce the mechanical assembly would, in effect, have to reverse engineer it, in order set up the equipment needed to reproduce it. Copying a digital artefact is as simple as typing:

cp old.one new.one

Copying an analogue artefact is vastly more difficult, and therefore there is little difference between slavish copying (which would invoke GPL-like restrictions), or reverse-engineering and re-manufacturing (which wouldn't). In this case, it's much more likely that the "cost" of GPL-like compliance would be greater than the benefits of having a GPL-free object.

So even if GPL-like licences are legally effective in the physical world, economics would tend to disfavour their use.

Designers, therefore, operating in the analogue realm may choose an openness model more akin to BSD that to GPL. Their challenge is to make this model work, and discourage free riders with a combination of moral pressure and a demonstration that playing by the community norms will be beneficial both to them, and to the community as a whole.

Designers and creators are increasingly able to benefit from the promise of the connected, social mode of creativity. The way was paved by free software pioneers, who skilfully hacked the copyright system to generate a commons which has not only, generated a huge global business, but also provided the software which runs devices from mobile phones through to the most powerful supercomputers. It provides the software which gives the developing world access to education, medical information, micro finance loans and enables them to participate in the knowledge economy on similar terms to the developed nations.

The challenge for designers and creators in other fields is to adapt the model of software development to their own field of work, and to counter the extensive efforts of incumbent beneficiaries of the broadcast era to use ever more draconian legislation to prop up the outmoded business models. Ultimately, the social mode will win: it takes one of humanity's defining characteristics, the fact that as animals we are highly social and community oriented, and uses it as the foundation of the entire structure. One-to-many works against this fundamental trait. Nature will ultimately triumph.

Open Design: Definition

An open design is:

0. The freedom to use the design, including making items based on it, for any purpose (freedom 0).

1. The freedom to study how the design works, and change it to make it do what you wish (freedom 1). Access to the underlying design documents is a precondition for this.

2. The freedom to redistribute copies of the design so you can help your neighbour (freedom 2).

3. The freedom to distribute copies of your modified versions of the design to others (freedom 3). By doing this you can give the whole community a chance to benefit from your changes. Access to the underlying design documents is a precondition for this.

(A version of the Free Software Foundation's "four freedoms" repurposed for designs by OHANDA – the Open Source Hardware and Design Alliance).

Rights And Licensing Schemes

The re-use of designs is governed mainly by copyright, design rights and patents. Traditional open licensing schemes have been based on copyright, as this is the main intellectual property right which impinges on software, the most fertile ground for openness.

Software licensing schemes include the GPL (which enforces copyleft) and BSD (which doesn't). A more comprehensive list of licences can be found at

http://www.opensource.org/licenses/index.html.

Software licences rarely work properly when applied to other works. For literary, graphic and musical works, the creative commons suite is more effective: www.creativecommons.org. They allow both copyleft (*share alike*) and non-copyleft options. They may work well when applied to underlying design documents, which are covered by copyright, and control the distribution of those documents, and the creation of physical objects from them, but their protection is unlikely to extend (depending on the jurisdiction) to the copying the physical object itself.

Creative Commons And Design Rights

Creative Commons licensing is fundamentally based on copyright, and there is little clarity or consensus on how they would operate in relation to design rights across the myriad different jurisdictions and types of right. Those designers operating purely in the realm of copyright will find that there is already an existing structure of support in terms of Creative Commons licences and associated communities. Where other forms of intellectual property impinge, the world is less developed. The Creative Commons licences are arguably sufficiently broadly drafted to cover unregistered design in certain circumstances, but because they were not drafted with design rights in mind, it cannot be assumed that the copying of a three-dimensional object will automatically fall within its scope.

Patents are specifically excluded from Creative Commons licenses: this, a designer can appear to be offering a design on an open basis using a CC license, but still withhold patents rights necessary for its manufacture or sale.

Andrew Katz has practised technology law for 20 years, and has been at Moorcrofts in the UK's Thames Valley for 14 of those. He is a Fellow of the Open Forum Academy and Free Software Foundation Europe and visiting lecturer on Free and Open Source Software at Queen Mary, University of London. He has lectured on open issues in London, Paris, New York, Boston, Seoul, Helsinki, Stockholm, Mangalia (Romania), Brussels, Amsterdam, Barcelona, Edinburgh, Oxford and Cambridge. He is on the core drafting team of the CERN Open Hardware licence. He acts for some of the world's leading free and open source software companies and projects. Andrew has more recently been involved in the rapidly expanding fields of open data and open hardware, and as well as speaking on legal issues at the Open Hardware Summit in New York in 2012, he co-opened the 2014 Open Hardware and Data Conference in Barcelona (the world's first legal conference specialising in open hardware and data).

Andrew is married with two children and lives in Oxfordshire. He's heavily involved in both the Oxford tech and music scenes and is passionate about live music: the grottier the venue, the better. He still codes occasionally, mainly Javascript and Python, although his favourite computer language will always be Pascal.

www.ingramcontent.com/pod-product-compliance
Lightning Source LLC
Chambersburg PA
CBHW051235050326
40689CB00007B/922